What are People Saying about *Picture*

"After having completed a first thorough reading of *'Pict...* thank you for having offered in it such **a wise, humane, and hopeful blueprint... ... ALL relationships, including those which pass through divorce**.

...
Thank you for the reminder.
-----Peter G., a grateful, very articulate *Picture Your Divorce* reader

"Dear Terry: Congratulations! The epic results are in for the **USA "Best Books 2011®"** Awards!
Your book has been honored as a "Finalist" in the "Parenting/Family: Divorce" category:
Picture Your Divorce: See How You Can Make the Right Divorce Decisions by Terry McNiff. Thank you for making The USA "Best Books 2011®" Awards one of the most successful mainstream book award programs in the United States....Regards,
-----Jeffrey Keen President & CEO JPX Media Group USABookNews.com InternationalBookAwards.com" **
www.usabooknews.com/bestbooks2012awards/bestbooks2011results.html

"Congratulations! We wanted to take a moment and again personally congratulate you on your achievement!
Picture Your Divorce **by Terry McNiff has been selected the FINALIST of the 2011 Indie Excellence® Award in the category of Divorce**.
The Indie Excellence Awards are reserved for the "best of the best" in books published in various genres. The criteria for recognition are stringent and include overall excellence in presentation. This award celebrates the highest achievements in independent press and self-publishing, a sector of the industry that has grown exponentially in recent years.... Sincerely,
------Ellen Reid, CEO National Indie Excellence® Awards "A Commitment to Excellence" *
www.indieexcellence.com/indie-results-2011.htm

"*Picture Your Divorce* -- the Book is **a must read for anyone thinking about or going through a divorce**. If that's you, you should read *Picture Your Divorce* as soon as possible.
Picture Your Divorce will save you time & money -- & possibly your sanity -- with easy-to-understand divorce decision diagrams. *Information you need that most attorneys won't give you*."
-----Karen A. Rhyne, Esq., an attorney since 1985, and a Board Certified Family Law Specialist since 1991; Adjunct Professor who taught Family Law courses quarterly at the University of California Irvine Extension Division from 1992 to 2005; Panelist: "Everything You Want to Know About Divorce". See www.michel-rhyne.com

Picture Your Divorce to See the Right Decisions

Decisions You Can Live With –
Without Regret –
Before, During & After Your Divorce

ISBN 978-0-9830627-5-2

Published in the U.S.A. by JP Reammard Publishing, 1895 Avenida Del Oro, #4422, Oceanside, California, 92056, 760-805-8081.

Please note that this book does not contain legal advice. This book contains legal and practical tools, pictures, and information only. The difference between legal advice and legal information is explained more fully in the section entitled "Disclaimers" near the back of this book, and below. Legal information is not a substitute for competent legal advice from an expert attorney. Legal information is general information that may or may not apply to a particular person in a particular situation. Legal advice is fact-specific advice that first requires at the very least a competent, expert attorney's complete knowledge, understanding and careful consideration of:

(1) all potentially relevant factual information about a particular individual's actual legal problem(s) and personal situation; and

(2) all of the actual law about procedure and substance in a particular location that may apply to a specific factual situation.

As a result, competent legal advice cannot be given without a complete factual interview of the individual person, that individual person's complete disclosure of all potentially pertinent facts, with a complete history, and that individual person's retained attorney having the time, opportunity, and expertise to render a fully-developed written legal opinion.

Dedicated to the Children

Of Divorce

Picture Your Divorce Contents

I.   Introduction

Why another book about divorce? This one is different. This divorce book gives you pictures. Pictures most clearly show you the issues, options, and likely consequences of the major decisions you're likely to face in your divorce. This book's pictures help you see your way to make better divorce decisions to benefit yourself and your loved ones.

Why Do I Believe This Book Teaching Better Divorce Decision-Making is Needed?

Experience Shows Many People Still Make Bad Decisions in their Divorces – Partly Because of Ignorance.

You may think making divorce decisions you can live with comfortably – which means without regrets and without anger – now & for the rest of your life – is not such a big deal. But, in my experience, practicing family law over 25 years, I can tell you that making good decisions under the stress of a divorce is a big deal. And it's not easy. In my experience, many people get it wrong – far too often. And they hurt because they decided wrong.

I have spent a great deal of time in courtrooms for many years observing people in their divorces make the same mistakes – over and over again. Usually, the one they hurt the most is themselves. Partly because of how righteous they feel, usually, when people in a divorce attack their spouse, as they do, far too often, they attack far too viciously. It pains me to watch how many people go through their divorce – in a public spectacle of hate and war they will eventually regret.

For over 25 years, I've sat in courtrooms for long periods waiting for my clients' divorce cases to be heard, and I've observed many others act out in their divorces. Over those many hours over many years I've repeatedly seen people who were not my clients unravel, attack, shoot themselves in the foot – and cause great pain to their families & themselves. It's painful to see. That repeated experience has made me wish I could do something to help those people.

For over 25 years, in those same courtrooms, I've repeatedly experienced seeing litigants who were not my clients – and sometimes their lawyers – express shock and horror at the outcome of their court hearing. They apparently failed to realize the potential – or most likely – consequences. I wished I could help those people too.

People going through divorce often seem to fail to understand how the facts and law look to an unbiased or objective observer. And, they often don't have a clue as to the potential

1

– or most likely – consequences. Far too often, I've observed people in their divorce become misguided, or fail to get good advice that could help them make good divorce decisions. This book is intended to help those people see – and learn – how to make good decisions in their divorce to avoid hurting themselves – and avoid hurting their loved ones.

Those litigants expressing or feeling shock or horror at the results of their court hearing also apparently failed to realize that a few things they controlled – or they should have known – converged to make a bad result likely:

- They failed to understand the basic key ideas or facts or factors that determine court outcomes

- They failed to develop reasonable expectations based on the potential – or most likely -- consequences

- They failed to understand they – or their attorney – could (with adequate, appropriate analysis and preparation ahead of time, i.e., long before their hearing):

  - Show the Court the key facts favoring them – and show why those facts mattered the most

  - Keep out of evidence key facts against them – or show why those facts didn't matter the most

  - Alternatively, if they couldn't do those 2 things, re-evaluate and consider settlement options

For over 25 years, I've also had the repeated experience of potential clients coming to me after their divorce, when they had been represented by someone else in their divorce, & then telling me they suffered from problems they needed my help to fix. Often, in the context of my asking how their divorce result or problem arose, they've asked themselves:

- "Why didn't I………………………………………(do the right thing)?"

- "Why did I……………………………………….(do the wrong thing)?"

Almost invariably, they answered "I don't know." "I wish I knew." "I didn't or couldn't see clearly."

Or, if they didn't think of the questions themselves, I almost always saw that to help them I needed to ask them:

- Why didn't you………………………………………..(do the right thing)?

- Why did you…………………………………………..(do the wrong thing)?

Almost invariably, they answered "I don't know." "I wish I knew." "I didn't or couldn't see clearly."

I've also had the repeated experience of potential clients coming to me after their divorce, when someone else had represented them in their divorce, and they had failed to solve a problem they could have and should have solved at the time of their divorce. Often, I've asked them:

- Why didn't you……………………………………..(solve this problem you could easily anticipate at the time of your divorce)?

- Why did you……………………………………..(at the time of your divorce, leave unresolved this problem you should have known would arise again later, causing you to re-live some of the pain of your divorce)?

Almost invariably, they answered: "I didn't know." "I didn't see I could have or should have resolved everything finally and fairly." "No one told me." "I didn't or couldn't see clearly."

Almost invariably, upon exploring the answers of these potential clients who needed help fixing their unresolved divorce problems, we determined together their unresolved problem arose from their ignorance about the issues, options, or potential consequences. No one could blame them. They were simply ignorant about what they didn't know. They didn't know what they didn't know. And what they didn't know, they needed to know – in order to make better decisions.

Most of the problems they suffered from during or after their divorce arose from their ignorance, or arose from inadequate thought in decision-making &/or planning to resolve issues in their divorce fairly and finally. As a result, they had to re-visit & re-engage in conflict with their formerly-loved one. Sometimes, they had to do it over and over again. And they found it painful. Some of them regretted what they had done or hadn't done, and they wished they could go back and fix it. Such regret is a powerfully negative force that disturbed some people for many years.

Sometimes, these people saw, through the benefit of hindsight, some of what they should have – or could have – done to make their divorce better, easier, or less stressful. In those instances, I heard a familiar refrain:

- If only I hadn't...........(done the wrong thing), my divorce would've been better.

- If only I had..............(done the right thing), my divorce would've been easier.

I've also had the repeated experience of hearing a person going through divorce wish she or he didn't have to endure a divorce. Many times, I've heard the person who initiated the divorce wish she or he had not initiated the divorce. They wish they could go back, and not get divorced. They wish they could reverse the decisions they made, or reverse the actions they took, that had brought them to the point they had reached, going through a painful divorce. But, once the divorce process starts, it's usually too late to go back. The train to divorce has left the station, and many times, that train becomes a runaway train that you can't get off.

Of course, these different experiences made me think, there has to be a better way for these people to succeed – or to reach a better result – in their divorce. There has to be a better way to help these people before they get to me, or need an attorney. There has to be a better way to help these people avoid regretting the actions they took, or failed to take, and the decisions they made, or failed to make, in their divorces. There has to be a better way to help these people avoid shock and horror at the outcome of their court hearing. Even if they can't afford to – or don't want to – hire a good attorney. And, there is a better way. More and better education on the realities and practicalities of divorce: the issues, the options or choices – and their likely consequences – can show these unfortunate people a better way.

I have had the good fortune to enjoy both sufficient education and experience to know a better way to divorce. More than 25 years' experience helping my clients get through one of the most difficult, prolonged, painful experiences in life reveals the key issues to consider in order to make good divorce decisions. More than 15 years' experience teaching other lawyers to be better lawyers – primarily in the practice of family law – reveals even more issues to consider in order to make better divorce decisions.

One of my teaching endeavors I have been fortunate to experience is an article I have written and revised each year for the last 15 years for the Los Angeles County Bar Association's Family Law Reference Book called "Family Law Techniques and Trial Tips". Writing an article advising divorce lawyers what they haven't been doing, and what they need to be doing, to help their clients, requires one to focus even more on divorce issues, options (or choices), and likely consequences. In other words, I haven't just been practicing family law for my own clients. Instead, I've also been observing and interviewing leading family law lawyers and judges to determine the best practices to achieve the best results – short-term and long-term. And, then I've given the answers; advising divorce attorneys how to do a better job of anticipating – and meeting the needs of their clients in divorce. I've incorporated into my teachings and my own practice with my clients many of the thoughts expressed here about a better way to divorce.

In looking back over my 25+ years of experience, with the benefit of hindsight, I realize that from my perspective, I want to help a lot more people than I am able to help just representing individual clients one on one. This book arises from those thoughts and experiences and my desire to help more people. The primary goal is to reach out, touch, and help those people who need help, and those people who maybe can't afford to or don't want to hire a divorce attorney, or at least an exceptional divorce attorney. I also believe this book can help people who have hired an attorney, but want to know more about the basic divorce issues, options, and consequences – or want to do what they can do to help themselves make good divorce decisions. In all situations and contexts, whether represented or unrepresented, divorcing people can and should learn more about divorce options, issues, and consequences. Then, they won't have later regrets.

Why Do People Make Bad Decisions in Their Divorces – Aside from their Own Ignorance?

Divorce is Stressful, Emotional, & Potentially Destructive – & Most People Can't See The Consequences.

The main reason many people get it wrong much of the time – making good decisions in their divorces – is partly because divorce is one of the most stressful experiences of life. The mental health professionals – psychologists, psychiatrists, counselors, therapists, etc. – generally agree that divorce is the 2nd most stressful life event. (The death of a really close loved one is usually deemed to be the most stressful.) The extreme stress of divorce often consumes or overwhelms many people.

Under great stress, we all have trouble making good decisions. We also have great trouble seeing the likely or potential consequences of our decisions. If we can even think or see clearly enough to actually try to consider the consequences of our decisions – most people don't or can't or won't. So, under severe stress, we tend to make decisions that create consequences we don't want. Consequences we didn't foresee.

Those consequences we don't want may be short-term consequences or long-term consequences. Suffering consequences we don't want – and didn't see ahead of time – can –

and often does – make us more upset, leading to more bad decisions. In my experience, bad decision-making in divorce can – and often does – become a vicious circle or cycle. Once it starts, it's hard to end it. When you also consider the likelihood your spouse will also make bad decisions or react badly to your bad decisions, you can see the vicious cycle of bad decisions tends to grow and perpetuate.

Good divorce decisions are decisions you can live with, and feel comfortable about, now, and long into the future. Good divorce decisions don't unnecessarily cause anyone pain. Making good divorce decisions requires you to realize first what else makes good divorce decision-making hard to do. So you won't make the same mistakes as other people.

There are many other reasons you'll find making good decisions in the stress of divorce is incredibly difficult, including the following reasons:

- **Almost everyone you know will claim to be an expert in divorce – and they won't hesitate to tell you what you should do**. Your friends and relatives almost all know someone who went through a divorce, or they went through it themselves, or they saw one in movies or tv. As a result of that experience, many think they're experts. And they're eager to share their expertise – and tell you what you should do. Much of the time the advice your friends and relatives give you is not helpful in the total scheme of things, not applicable to your facts or the law in your state, and not consistent. Your case is unique. All of that usually bad advice from others who usually mean well makes it harder – and more confusing – for you to make good decisions.

- **Divorce is an ongoing stressful experience – without a certain beginning or end**. Sometimes, it's hard to tell when a divorce begins. Or ends. Sure, we can tell when someone files for divorce. But, they'll later tell their ex (or anyone who will listen) that their ex made the divorce certain, or necessary, by something their ex did – days, weeks, months, or years before they actually filed for divorce. And, it's hard to tell when divorce ends, because some people will fight about it for years. Many people will fight with their ex long after they actually get a divorce. In various ways, divorce is unlike many other stressful life events, such as the death of a loved one, loss of a job, moving away, etc.

- **While your divorce is going on, it's not so easy to see that your judgment and decision-making ability are impaired**. Having been divorced, and having observed many people getting a divorce, I can tell you people going through a divorce don't usually know how impaired they are during their divorce. They usually can't see the depth and breadth of their impairment until about a year or more after they get divorced. Some people never see or learn that painful fact. And they keep repeating their mistakes over and over – causing themselves and loved ones great pain.

- **<u>Nuances of divorce law can make getting a divorce complex</u>**. Divorce law, like a lot of other law, is complex. There are many rules, exceptions to the main rules, exceptions to the exceptions, presumptions that sometimes trump the rules, exceptions, or evidence – and repeated changes to all of them. Legislators seem to feel the need to change divorce laws in various ways – over and over again – in the name of progress, social engineering, improvement, etc. And different courts interpret the same laws, or similar laws, differently. Sometimes, courts interpret laws in a way most people, including the experts, didn't think possible or likely. On top of that, human affairs and relationships are complex. Applying complex rules to complex human interactions and circumstances sometimes leads to unanticipated and unintended results. It is no wonder that a person untrained in the law often finds great difficulty or challenges in trying to fully understand divorce law.

- **<u>Love and hate, the 2 most prominent emotions in divorce, can vex and confound the best of us</u>**. The more emotional we get, the harder it becomes for us to make good decisions. Our emotions interfere with our thinking. Since divorces are usually very emotional experiences, and strong emotions make it hard to make good decisions, you should think at least twice – before you act. And, you should thoroughly explore the potential options and likely consequences of your actions and choices – before you act.

- **<u>Popular culture urges you to get it fixed now – just do it – while good divorce decisions and results can take time</u>**. Popular culture pounds to the beat of fix it now and do it now. Popular culture creates and reinforces the notion we don't have to put up with anything we don't like. Popular culture demands we take immediate, aggressive action to fix or eliminate anything that bothers us. But, good divorce decisions and results require time and mature consideration. This culture clash creates and makes more likely rash divorce decisions – including the decision to divorce. Quickly.

- **<u>It's doubly difficult to make divorce decisions that turn out to be good for us – and for our family – both short-term </u>**(solving an immediate problem)**<u> and long-term</u>** (not creating trouble for years later). For at least a couple of reasons. First, it's hard to <u>picture</u> both the short-term and long-term consequences. Second, it's hard to <u>serve</u> simultaneously both the short-term and long-term consequences. What is good or right in the short term may not be good or right for the long term. And vice versa.

I'm sure those reading this book can think of more reasons why divorce decision-making is so difficult. But the point is – divorce decision-making is incredibly difficult. Picturing divorce decisions, options, and consequences can help you see everything more clearly.

Why (or How) are Pictures Going to Help Change Bad Decision-Making in Divorce?

Pictures are 5-6 times More Effective as Learning and Decision-Making Tools.

Scientists tell us we learn more from pictures. Pictures can be 5 to 6 times more effective than words alone. Our brains work in pictures and associations; so pictures help our brains see things more clearly. Pictures tell a thousand words. And, with pictures, you won't get lost or bored after a few, or many, pages. You'll see more, differently, each time you look at the pictures. You can add to or subtract from the pictures in this book, and you can make your own pictures.

Pictures are the best way for you to see how you can make divorce decisions you can live with –without severe regrets and without anger. Seeing is believing – and understanding.

Pictures also help you use this guidebook as a quick reference to refer to again and again, to help you reach your best decisions throughout the process of your divorce. With the pictures in this guide, you won't have to search in vain for a particular thought or subject – or the guidance you seek. You'll find the reference you're looking for right away in the list of pictures in the Table of Contents. You can readily see it all in a series of pictures.

I've used pictures for many years to help my clients and I make the difficult decisions in their cases, and in my practice. The right pictures do make it much easier to see – and evaluate and choose – the key options and consequences. Based on what the scientists tell us about how our brains work, these pictures should work for many people – most of the time. If they don't, at least I've spread the word about the value and benefit of your own pictures.

The main question divorce experience presents to us is:

How can we make divorce decision-making easier & better?

The answer is 3-fold:

1. **Identify the Main Problems in Divorce** –the key things most people struggle with most – from A to Z.

2. **Picture the Divorce Decisions Options and Consequences**.

3. **Empower You, the Divorcing Person, to Draw Your Own Divorce Decision-Making Pictures**.

Doing all 3 of those things – identifying, picturing, and empowering – is what makes this book different from all of the other 100's of books on divorce. Doing all 3 of these things is also what makes this book most useful to the person going through the painful ordeal of divorce. Divorce doesn't have to be so painful. All you need to do is know more about the divorce process, and think more clearly. And you need help to think more clearly, and to see more clearly the options and likely or potential consequences of your decisions.

Learning experts tell us:

- **We learn the most by doing**.

- **We learn the least by only listening or hearing**.

- **We learn somewhere in the middle by seeing –less than we learn by doing, but much more than we learn by only listening**.

So, it's the seeing and doing that is the focus of this book. In order to help you see more clearly, I've drawn basic pictures of the main problems in divorce – the things that cause the most trouble for most people – and your potential options and likely or potential consequences for dealing with those problems. The pictures help you with the seeing. And the pictures also help you with the doing.

The doing involves you creating your own pictures. You can add to – or subtract from – the pictures in this book – or create your own pictures entirely from scratch. I have left plenty of space in most of the pictures here for you to fill in the details or other things that matter most to you. You can also subtract or delete or cross out the things in the pictures here that you know or believe do not apply to you. It's up to you how you do it. You should just get to the doing. And this book gives you a head start over everyone else.

My main point is that you can work your way through your divorce best by starting with these pictures. Then **create your own pictures showing your options or choices – and**

their likely or potential consequences. Completing that exercise in each instance will usually help you see more clearly – and make better choices.

I've done what I believe I can to make this book and the pictures accurate and representative of the main issues you're likely to face in divorce. That should make the pictures most useful to the vast majority of people getting divorces. The vast majority of people getting divorces are doing so without the benefit of attorneys. As a result, I've created this book to give these people a general guide to most of the issues, options and consequences of divorce. With the benefit of the lessons I have learned in over 25 years of divorce practice.

Your particular answers to the issues facing you in your divorce – and the key options and consequences for you – lie at least partly within you.[1] You just need to explore – and see the key options and likely consequences for yourself.

You don't need a computer or a fancy computer program to draw your own pictures. You can use a pencil and paper to draw your own pictures. Or you can add and subtract from the pictures I've provided you here. It's up to you.

You have choices. Your choices create consequences. And if you want good consequences, then you need to choose wisely.

---

[1] Since a lawyer wrote this book, and lawyers are famous for their disclaimers, the book comes with vast disclaimers. Please carefully review the Disclaimers section, inserted at the end of the book, for your convenience.

Please remember that any person going through a divorce needs to keep a sense of humor. A healthy sense of humor will help you through the roughest times. As a result, the author has injected a bit of humor into this book. Of course, that's risky, because most people consider divorce to be a huge negative. If you happen to find anything in this book offensive or not to your liking, please understand that is probably just a result of the author being not so great at his attempts at humor. And, for gosh sakes, don't take it personally! Laugh once in a while. It's good for you.

This book also comes with 2 serious caveats or warnings upfront.

1. If you are the victim of domestic violence or abuse, get yourself to a domestic violence shelter. Don't stop to read this book, or try to work things out. Get yourself protected first. This book is much less useful to people who are in a relationship with a domestic violence or abuse perpetrator. Domestic violence or abuse changes the rules almost completely, and in that situation, protecting yourself and your children becomes the highest priority.

2. This book focuses on children of divorce in many instances to help their divorcing parents picture the consequences for their children. Children can become victimized by divorce and the decisions their parents make in divorce, and I want to help both the children and their parents to avoid becoming victimized by the divorce. I believe sharing my experience can help both children and their parents.

II.   Pictures For Your Divorce from A to Z.

A.   Attorneys – Do You Want or Need One? If so, How Do You Pick the Best One For You?

1.   Do You Need an Attorney? If so, do you want representation or consultation?

The first issue is attorneys, a subject near and dear to my heart. The first question is whether you need one. Despite my bias, I can tell you that you don't always need an attorney.

You particularly do not need an attorney if any or all of the items set forth in the following picture are true for you. So whether you get an attorney is up to you. If you decide to get an attorney, you need to realize selecting the right attorney for yourself is critical to your success. You also need to decide if you want full legal representation or just have an attorney to consult.

The right attorney for you can usually save money and time, and get you a better result.

The wrong attorney for you will almost always cost you a great deal in money, time, or results. Sometimes, all three.

So, the best thing you can do if you decide you want to use an attorney is to choose wisely. Choosing wisely requires you to take your time & do all of the following things first:

- *Research Potential Attorneys for the right qualifications & traits*
- *Interview at least 3 Attorneys & Compare them to each other*
- *Use Objective Criteria or Factors to Compare the Attorneys*
- *Choose the Most Experienced Attorney You can afford – because the law is complex, the best decisions require excellent judgment, and experience is the best teacher*

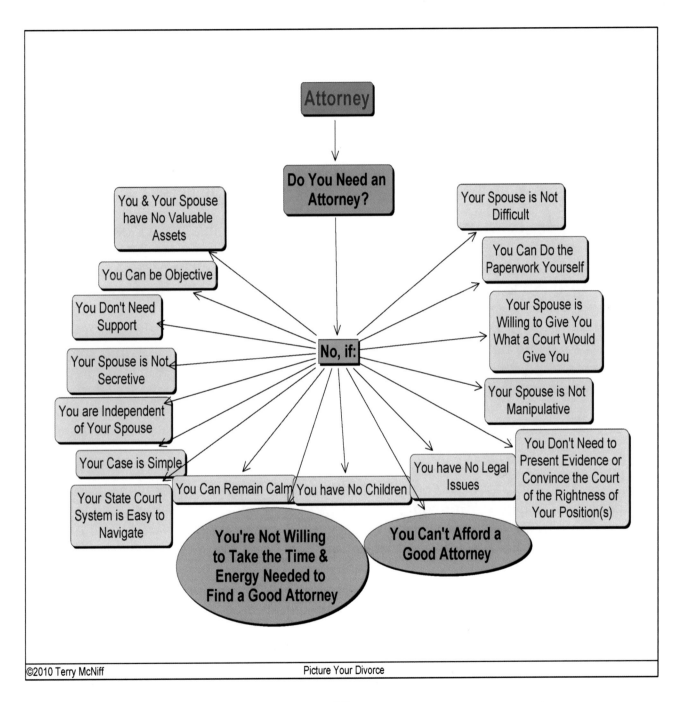

Attorney

Do You Need an Attorney?

No, if:

You & Your Spouse have No Valuable Assets

You Can be Objective

You Don't Need Support

Your Spouse is Not Secretive

You are Independent of Your Spouse

Your Case is Simple

Your State Court System is Easy to Navigate

You Can Remain Calm

You have No Children

You have No Legal Issues

Your Spouse is Not Difficult

You Can Do the Paperwork Yourself

Your Spouse is Willing to Give You What a Court Would Give You

Your Spouse is Not Manipulative

You Don't Need to Present Evidence or Convince the Court of the Rightness of Your Position(s)

You're Not Willing to Take the Time & Energy Needed to Find a Good Attorney

You Can't Afford a Good Attorney

2. An Alternative View or Picture: Find the View or Picture That's Best for You

Since we'll be working with pictures a lot in this book, I want to explain some of the key things I've learned about visualizing ideas and information.

One of the first key things I've learned is that people view things differently. This is true even when the thing they are viewing is laid out in detail in a picture or diagram.

For instance, the picture on the page preceding this page looks perfectly clear to me.
That picture starts with the subject on top – giving me an immediate orientation.
The second line or box of that picture (moving down from the top) states the issue simply.
The third line or box of that picture answers the question.
The remaining boxes reflect caveats or exceptions to the general answer.
The main purpose for these boxes is to give you, the reader, additional information.
The reader may choose to accept that information, or parts of it – or reject some or all of it.
The main point is to include the most relevant factors in order to best answer the question.

However, for some people, the picture on the page preceding this page is not as clear as it could be. For some people, the same information expressed in a different way – as in the picture following this page – is vastly more clear. If neither view is clear, find or make a different picture that is best for you.

I'm not an expert in things spatial – so I won't purport to explain the difference. I only note the difference so that those who experience the views differently than me realize:
- There are different ways to view the same reality
- Each person needs to find the view that works best for them, and use it

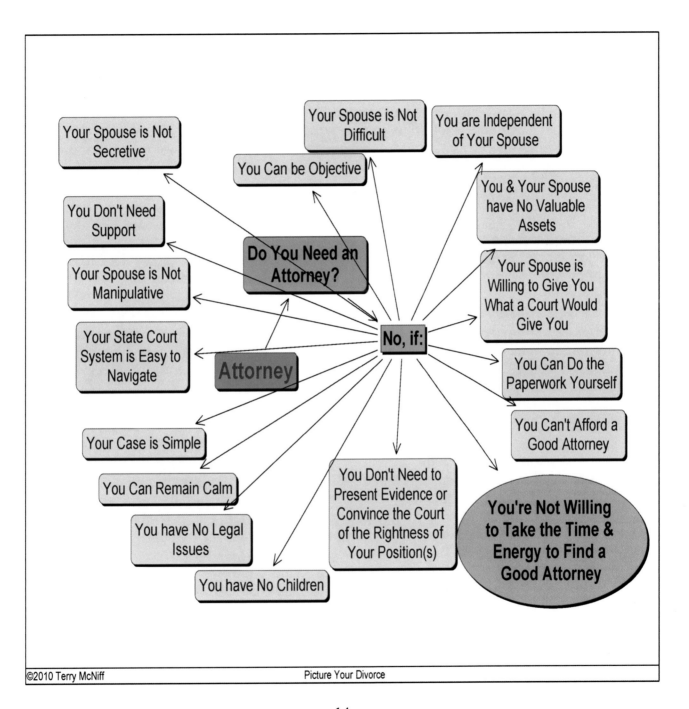

Your Spouse is Not Secretive

Your Spouse is Not Difficult

You are Independent of Your Spouse

You Don't Need Support

You Can be Objective

Do You Need an Attorney?

You & Your Spouse have No Valuable Assets

Your Spouse is Not Manipulative

Your Spouse is Willing to Give You What a Court Would Give You

Your State Court System is Easy to Navigate

Attorney

No, if:

You Can Do the Paperwork Yourself

Your Case is Simple

You Can't Afford a Good Attorney

You Can Remain Calm

You have No Legal Issues

You Don't Need to Present Evidence or Convince the Court of the Rightness of Your Position(s)

You're Not Willing to Take the Time & Energy to Find a Good Attorney

You have No Children

Picture Your Divorce

3. Where Do You Find a Good Attorney, If You've Decided You Want or Need One?

The best place to find an attorney is from someone who knows a good attorney. If you happen to be fortunate enough to know a good attorney in a field of law other than divorce, or a good divorce attorney in another location, you should ask them for recommendations. Usually, a good attorney in one field or location knows good attorneys in other fields or locations.

Sometimes, a person who has been through a divorce knows at least which of the 2 (or sometimes more) attorneys in their divorce did a good job. Ask the people you know who went through a divorce or who knows someone who went through a divorce. Talk to those you respect most. Thoroughly check out any attorneys recommended to you. Ask questions.

You can also find a good attorney by conducting your own research. The sources of such research are as vast as the Internet. In other words, there is a huge universe of information available. The problem for you will be to reduce that information to the most reliable sources. I identified the most reliable sources on the picture following. Probe and evaluate them yourself.

Before hiring any attorney, please make sure you look them up on their State Bar profile on the website of the State Bar for the State in which you reside. The State Bar in most states regulates attorneys and licenses attorneys to practice. Most State Bars will report on their website at least some basic information about every attorney practicing law in that state. That information includes the date they were licensed to practice, certified specialties, if any, and any discipline, including suspension, revocation, probation, etc. That information should be the bare minimum you obtain before you decide among several attorneys.

Be wary of websites recommending or rating attorneys. Many online recommendations or ratings are the result of advertising – i.e., money – or membership, rather than objective merit.

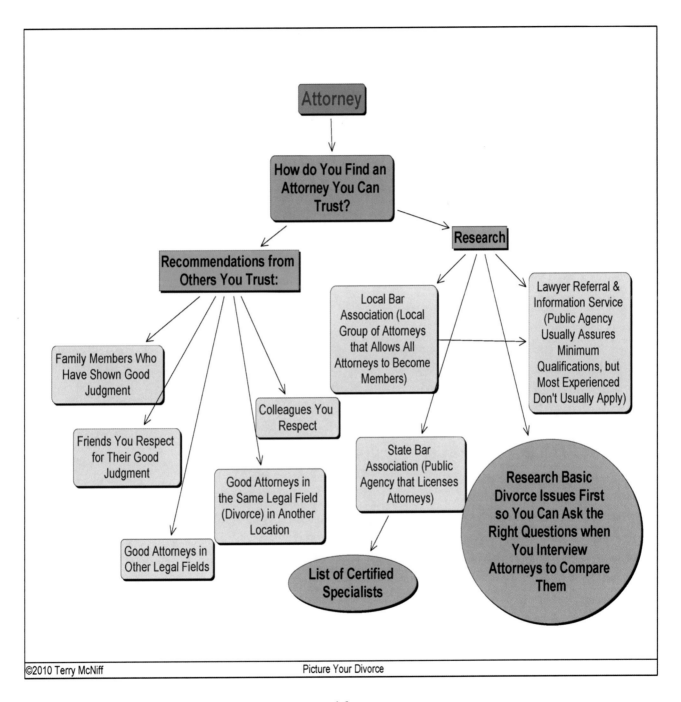

Picture Your Divorce

4. Warning Signs – Attorneys to Avoid

Like anything else I might suggest to help you succeed in your divorce, the suggestion about how to find the right attorney for you comes with caveats and warnings. If the potential attorney you are considering hiring shows you from the get-go the attorney lacks objectivity or lacks judgment, run away! The main quality a good attorney offers, and the main benefit a good attorney provides to you, is objectivity and judgment. If they don't possess good judgment, or if they're not objective, you don't need them. And, you don't want them.

You should avoid any attorney who has been disciplined by the State Bar or a Court for doing things harmful to a Client. You can usually learn that info on the State Bar website.

If the attorney you are considering practices in several subject areas of the law, you're probably better off with someone else. There are exceptions to this rule, such as attorneys in small towns who practice a variety of legal subjects because there aren't enough attorneys or potential clients to specialize in each subject. But, for the most part, attorneys who dabble in several subjects in the law are jacks of all trades, masters of none.

If the attorneys you are considering advertise excessively, or promote themselves excessively, you should probably avoid those attorneys. Attorneys who advertise or promote themselves excessively generally need to advertise or promote themselves to get business. In other words, they aren't good enough to get business the old-fashioned way, by word of mouth from satisfied clients.

Similarly, you don't need an attorney whose office is so lavish as to be a monument to the attorney. Someone has to pay for all that lavishness, and that someone includes you.

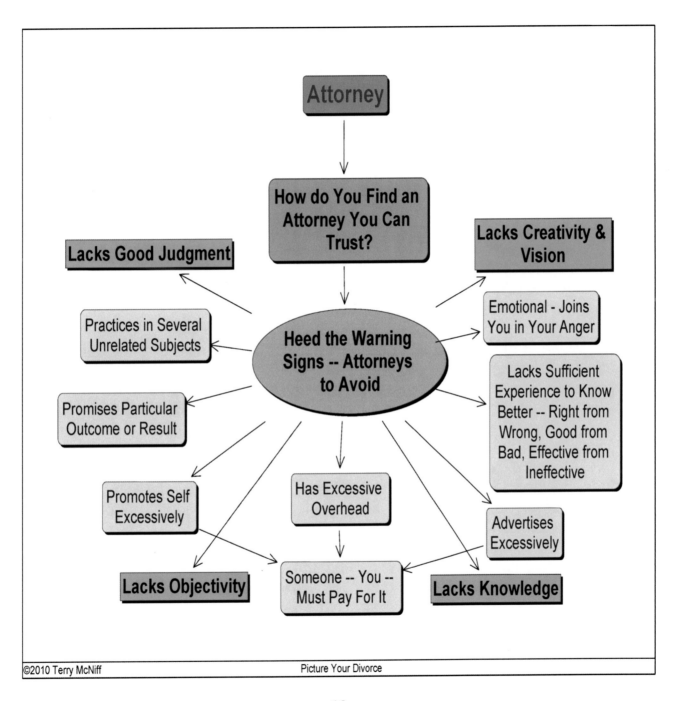

Picture Your Divorce

5. What Traits are Critical in an Attorney? How Do You Choose the Right Attorney?

One of the most desirable traits of an attorney is that the attorney be a specialist. If the attorney is certified by a state licensing agency as a specialist, that is far better than an attorney who calls herself a specialist, but is not officially recognized as a specialist. A specialty certified by an objective agency is proof of the attorney's experience in the field. You want the most experienced attorney you can get. The most experienced attorney knows the most.

Similarly, you should prefer for yourself an attorney who educates other attorneys about the subject of family law or divorce. Attorneys who educate other attorneys usually have gained the respect of others and a grasp of the subject far beyond those who do not teach the law.

One of the other most desirable traits of an attorney is that the attorney be objective and honest with you. If you talk to any divorce judge, they can tell you that the clients who create the most problems and incur the most expense are the people with the most unreasonable expectations. Unreasonable expectations come from lack of objectivity – or ignorance.

If you perceive either lack of objectivity or ignorance from your attorney, you hired the wrong attorney. If a potential attorney for your divorce tells you they'll solve all your problems exactly the way you want them solved, get up out of your chair, and walk out. Quickly.

Before hiring any attorney for yourself, you should interview several attorneys. Interviewing several attorneys gives you several advantages. First, you can see whether someone has the necessary expertise. Second, you can judge for yourself the individual attorney's judgment and objectivity – and compare them to others. Third, you can see which of several attorneys feels best – someone you can work with comfortably so you can best succeed.

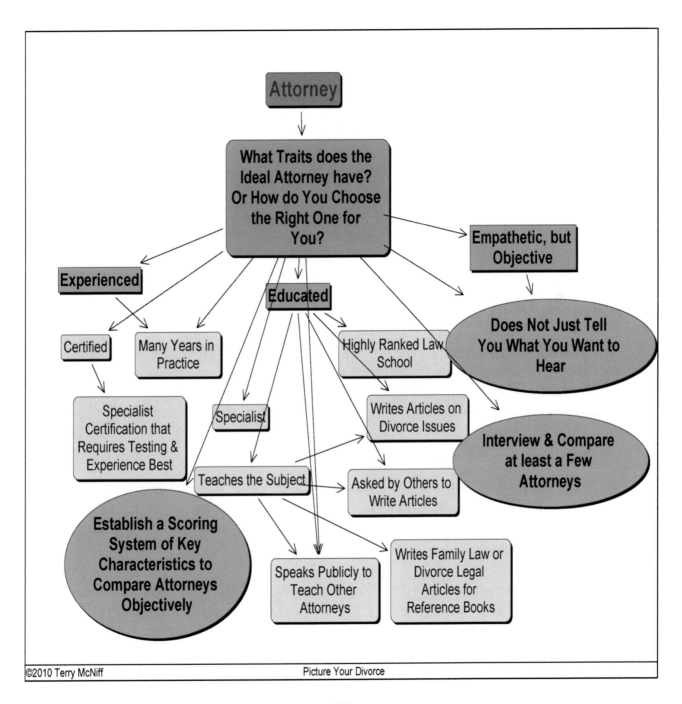

Picture Your Divorce

20

6. Another Alternative View: All Ideas About Attorneys in 1 Picture

People see pictures differently. Some people need to see all of the pictures or concepts or ideas concerning a particular subject on 1 page – or in 1 picture. These people find they make their best decisions when they can see all concepts together. These people sometimes find they experience a synergistic effect between the concepts when all concepts are together.

A synergistic effect here is one in which the ideas expressed work together to trigger your mind to bring to your consciousness other related ideas. The resulting synergy creates a greater total result or understanding than any things working alone – without the other things. For these people, the picture following contains all of the pictures so far – together on 1 page.

Some people see things more clearly with different colors. Some people may see things more clearly with different colors than those set forth in the following picture – or the other pictures in this guide. If you're one of those people, feel free to experiment with colors so you can find the colors that work best for you. The picture following, like each picture in this guide, is merely an example of 1 way to picture these ideas to help you see & paint your own pictures.

Some people may see ideas or things to do more clearly in a list format – rather than in a picture. If you're one of these people, feel free to turn any of these pictures into your own to do list. If you make a list, you probably want to rank order the to dos in some order or priority.

Since the pictures in this guide are examples for your personal use, I left space on the page for you to add the issues that matter to you. For instance, you may have thought of some questions you really want to ask potential attorneys. Feel free to add those questions to this picture. Whatever works for you, to help you make better decisions easier, you should do.

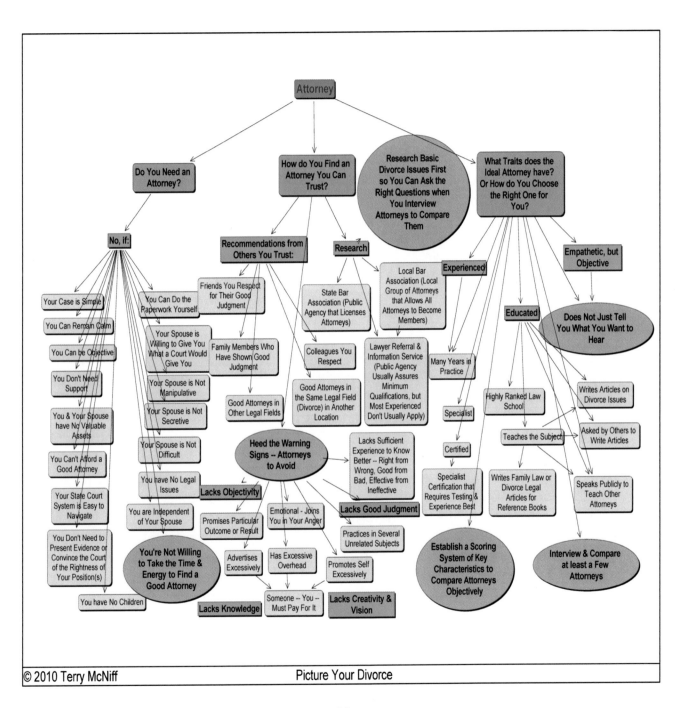

Attorney

Do You Need an Attorney?

No, if:
- Your Case is Simple
- You Can Remain Calm
- You Can be Objective
- You Don't Need Support
- You & Your Spouse have No Valuable Assets
- You Can't Afford a Good Attorney
- Your State Court System is Easy to Navigate
- You Don't Need to Present Evidence or Convince the Court of the Rightness of Your Position(s)
- You have No Children

How do You Find an Attorney You Can Trust?

Recommendations from Others You Trust:
- Friends You Respect for Their Good Judgment
- You Can Do the Paperwork Yourself
- Your Spouse is Willing to Give You What a Court Would Give You
- Family Members Who Have Shown Good Judgment
- Your Spouse is Not Manipulative
- Your Spouse is Not Secretive
- Your Spouse is Not Difficult
- You have No Legal Issues
- You are Independent of Your Spouse
- Good Attorneys in Other Legal Fields

Lacks Objectivity

You're Not Willing to Take the Time & Energy to Find a Good Attorney

Research

Research Basic Divorce Issues First so You Can Ask the Right Questions when You Interview Attorneys to Compare Them

- State Bar Association (Public Agency that Licenses Attorneys)
- Colleagues You Respect
- Good Attorneys in the Same Legal Field (Divorce) in Another Location
- Local Bar Association (Local Group of Attorneys that Allows All Attorneys to Become Members)
- Lawyer Referral & Information Service (Public Agency Usually Assures Minimum Qualifications, but Most Experienced Don't Usually Apply)

Heed the Warning Signs -- Attorneys to Avoid
- Promises Particular Outcome or Result
- Advertises Excessively
- Emotional - Joins You in Your Anger
- Has Excessive Overhead
- Someone -- You -- Must Pay For It
- Practices in Several Unrelated Subjects
- Promotes Self Excessively
- Lacks Sufficient Experience to Know Better -- Right from Wrong, Good from Bad, Effective from Ineffective

Lacks Good Judgment

Lacks Knowledge

Lacks Creativity & Vision

What Traits does the Ideal Attorney have? Or How do You Choose the Right One for You?

Experienced
- Many Years in Practice
- Specialist
- Certified
- Specialist Certification that Requires Testing & Experience Best

Educated
- Highly Ranked Law School
- Teaches the Subject
- Writes Family Law or Divorce Legal Articles for Reference Books

Empathetic, but Objective

Does Not Just Tell You What You Want to Hear
- Writes Articles on Divorce Issues
- Asked by Others to Write Articles
- Speaks Publicly to Teach Other Attorneys

Establish a Scoring System of Key Characteristics to Compare Attorneys Objectively

Interview & Compare at least a Few Attorneys

Picture Your Divorce

22

B.   Beginning Your Divorce.

1.   Before Beginning Your Divorce – Make Sure There's No Hope for Your Marriage.

Before you consider – or decide – to divorce your spouse, you should first consider and thoroughly analyze whether there is hope for your marriage. Analyze the reason or reasons for you to stay in your marriage. And work on your marriage.

I can't tell you how many times a spouse has told me after their divorce – and sometimes during their divorce – that they wished they had tried to save their marriage. You don't know what you've got till it's gone. So, I review these thoughts with my potential clients – and send them home to do their homework to make sure they know what they want. Before they begin.

The first thing to do for your homework before you begin your divorce is to picture what it will be like if your marriage is gone. List or identify all of the things that are good in your marriage – the advantages or benefits of your marriage to your spouse. Next, picture those good things gone. Next, picture or identify all of the bad things in your marriage that a divorce will solve – the disadvantages or deficits or defects in your marriage.

Now, put the 2 lists together – as a T-chart, or a picture, or some other way that allows you to see it all clearly. Then, evaluate what is most important, least important, or not important. Next, evaluate what you can work on to strengthen or improve your relationship. Then, consider how to convince your spouse to join with you to do the things necessary or appropriate to strengthen or improve your relationship. You don't know what your spouse may or may not be willing to try to do – unless and until you ask, gently, positively, without blame. You could be surprised. If your spouse refuses, then you'll take comfort knowing you tried everything first.

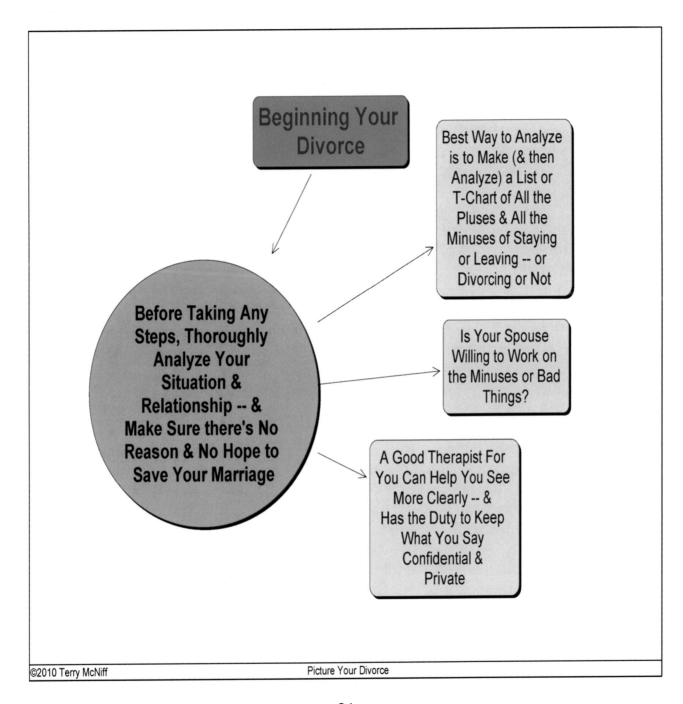

Beginning Your Divorce

Before Taking Any Steps, Thoroughly Analyze Your Situation & Relationship -- & Make Sure there's No Reason & No Hope to Save Your Marriage

Best Way to Analyze is to Make (& then Analyze) a List or T-Chart of All the Pluses & All the Minuses of Staying or Leaving -- or Divorcing or Not

Is Your Spouse Willing to Work on the Minuses or Bad Things?

A Good Therapist For You Can Help You See More Clearly -- & Has the Duty to Keep What You Say Confidential & Private

Picture Your Divorce

2. Study, Plan & Prepare So You Know What To Do – Before Your Divorce Begins.

Many people begin their divorce in a fit of anger. Those people miss the opportunity to picture the best divorce – and then get the best divorce. We all realize that when we act in a fit of anger or rage, we usually don't act in our own best self-interest. So, avoid acting in anger.

If you want to minimize trouble in your divorce, the best thing to do is to study the options available. There are options about how to proceed, or procedural options. There are also options about substance. (Please see Legal Issues Overview below for more information.) Consult an experienced attorney confidentially to check out the options and how they work.

These days, you can also check out divorce options on the web. Just make sure you distinguish between for-profit websites and non-profit websites. The non-profit sites that don't recommend particular attorneys, & don't have ads, are the best sites for accurate, unbiased information. (Please see the Bibliography, Useful References & Links at the end.)

For instance, most courts have self-help websites that will offer a variety of information and references. You can trust most court websites for the basic information they provide. They won't answer all your questions, but they will give you basic information. And usually, they will give you the basic information you need in a straightforward fashion – without any ads or hype.

The for-profit sites or recommending websites will generally direct you to the attorneys who paid them a fee. Sometimes, the fee is in the form of membership in a club. Whatever the designation, of one thing you can be certain – the members in any club or group will protect other members of their club or group first, foremost, and always. So, be wary of clubs.

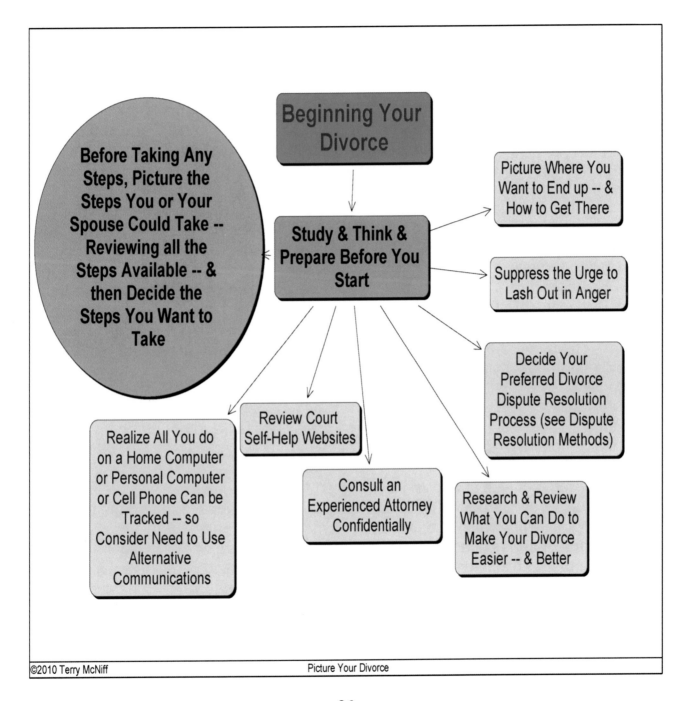

Beginning Your Divorce

Before Taking Any Steps, Picture the Steps You or Your Spouse Could Take -- Reviewing all the Steps Available -- & then Decide the Steps You Want to Take

Study & Think & Prepare Before You Start

Picture Where You Want to End up -- & How to Get There

Suppress the Urge to Lash Out in Anger

Decide Your Preferred Divorce Dispute Resolution Process (see Dispute Resolution Methods)

Realize All You do on a Home Computer or Personal Computer or Cell Phone Can be Tracked -- so Consider Need to Use Alternative Communications

Review Court Self-Help Websites

Consult an Experienced Attorney Confidentially

Research & Review What You Can Do to Make Your Divorce Easier -- & Better

　　　Picture Your Divorce

3. Take Steps to Protect Yourself – Before You Begin Your Divorce.

After you complete your initial study of divorce, you should take certain steps to protect yourself. The steps you need to take to protect yourself and your loved ones depend on your personal situation. For example, in every divorce, you'll need to gather financial information.

If you are in a relationship involving violence or abuse, you need to remove yourself physically first. Find a shelter. A shelter can be a safe house provided by a non-profit group. Or a shelter can be someone you know, a friend or relative. You need to remove yourself physically – and stay removed physically – in order to protect yourself, and to successfully picture your divorce. You can't think logically or objectively – or protect yourself – when you're trapped in an abusive situation.

If you are not in a violent or abusive situation, you still need to protect yourself. Even in the best situations, the other spouse may often do things, sooner or later, to cause you pain. If your spouse has all the money or income, he or she may cut you off financially. If you are the one without money or income, see if you can shelter some money before you start your divorce. Carefully consider other potential steps you can take or potential resources that may help you.

You can also take basic steps to protect yourself even if you are not dependent on your spouse. For example, one thing that often happens during the divorce is that the spouse who remains in the family home causes cherished things to disappear. That act, or series of acts, is extremely difficult to prove. They'll usually say you took it with you – and, just for spite, may claim that your false accusation against them proves you are bad or nasty or horrible. As strange as that may seem, it happens. People make stuff up. So, protect yourself, in this particular instance, by safeguarding cherished belongings or heirlooms.

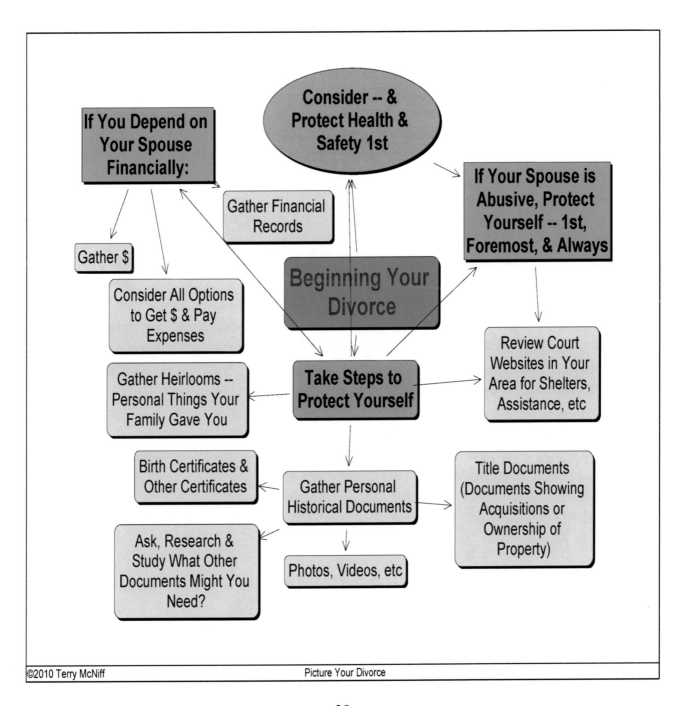

4. Decide the Time, Place & Manner of Informing Your Spouse – Before You Begin.

Many people leave to chance the time, place and manner of informing their spouses. Or, they let someone else decide this critical issue. Or, they let the first step be hurtful. Without thinking about it – or, what it can mean in the entire scheme of things. That is a mistake.

The first step you take is likely to be a step your spouse – and perhaps many others – will remember for a long time. So, consider – before you do anything – how you want others to remember that first step you took.

Also, consider that if you want to resolve your divorce peacefully, then your first step should be peaceful. Usually, the most peaceful first step occurs in the presence of someone else – a friend or family member whom both you and your spouse trust, or a good therapist or counselor, or someone similar. Consider who may help you make that first step peaceful.

One of the worst ways to begin – if you hope to divorce your spouse peacefully, and you don't actually need something immediately from your spouse or the court – is to file with the court and serve on your spouse a court application or motion demanding or requesting immediate court relief and a hearing. If you want to make your spouse feel defensive and under attack, that action will do it.

If you are on the receiving end of a court application or divorce filing – consider your first step just as carefully. You don't have to do or say the first thing that comes to mind. You can be smarter than that, and think through your options – and their consequences – before you react. You can choose how you're going to be, and what you do, from beginning to end.

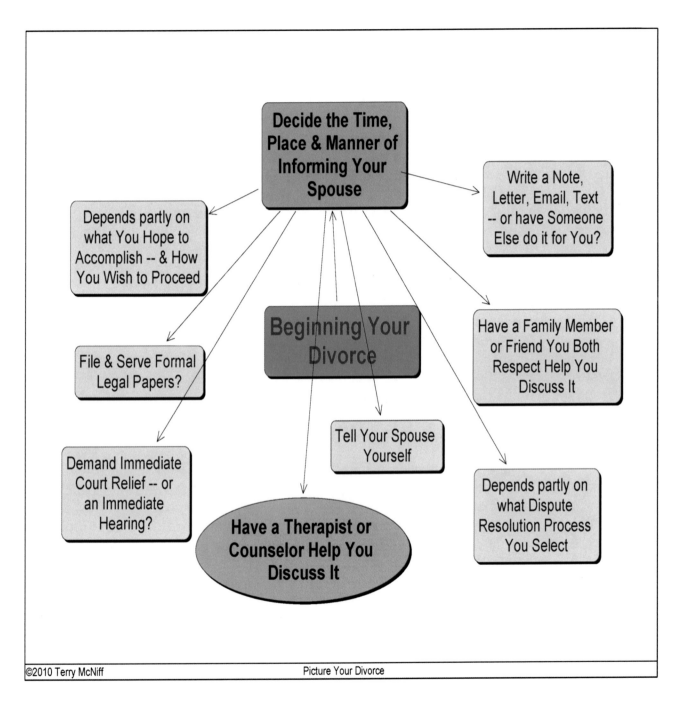

Picture Your Divorce

30

5. Beginning Your Divorce – All Views & Ideas Together for Those Who See Synergistically.

Before you begin your divorce, you need to take steps to protect yourself – from yourself. You can become your own worst enemy in your divorce. For example, you can become your own worst enemy by announcing your threatening intentions or actions – or threats of what you intend to do to your spouse. This can be harmful even if you think you're just blowing off steam. You could be recorded. You could be observed by witnesses. Family and friends can become witnesses. You could be the object of a request for restraining orders.

People in a divorce often mistakenly trust the wrong friends or family with their troubles. The friends or family you confide in about your divorce may be talking to your spouse. Sometimes, when a friend or family member is talking to your spouse, they feel like they are doing you a favor. Sometimes, they think they're protecting you. Sometimes, they think they can help you, perhaps as sort of a friendly intermediary. But, regardless of their intentions, your friends or family could say or do things that prove to be harmful to you in your divorce. And cost you dearly, or cause you pain. So, you should stop that from happening.

Also, you should realize that your spouse may be tracking you or spying on you. Your spouse may have installed software tracking on your computer – or your phone – or both. That software may tell your spouse every website you visit. That software may track every keystroke. That software may give your spouse a copy of every e-mail you send – or receive. If your spouse has that type of software, or access to the computer you use, you may be telegraphing to your spouse your every move. Your spouse may also be eavesdropping, physically or electronically. You need to take steps to make sure you know what you may be telling your spouse.

Any of your communication devices or sites or methods can – and will – be used against you. For instance, many people in a divorce have found useful information on the social media pages of their spouse, their spouse's family, their spouse's friends, and most of all, their spouse's significant other, i.e., their spouse's boyfriend or girlfriend. So, beware what you -- & friends – say in e-mail, in text messages, and in social media, like Facebook, MySpace, online forums, etc. The safest thing to do is to assume your spouse will or can get almost any communication. Their likelihood of doing so is a function of their determination, knowledge, and resources. A good rule to live by in these circumstances is that if you or others post something about you that you'd feel ashamed of or have a hard time defending in court, your spouse or ex is likely to find out that information. Don't you think that once they find it, they'll also find a way to use it against you?

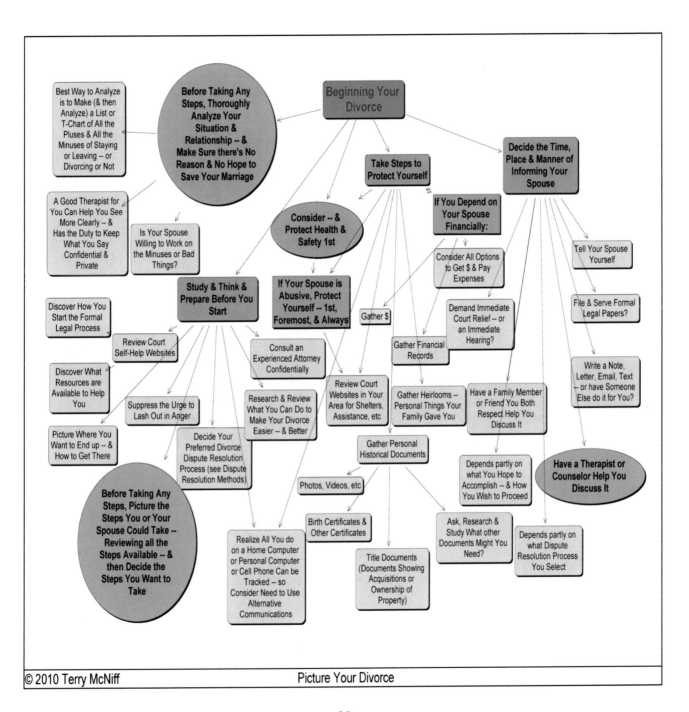

Picture Your Divorce

32

C.   Children.

1.   Your Children Suffer Most When You Fight With Their Other Parent.

Children suffer in a divorce. There is no escaping that fact. But:

- You are 1 of the 2 main characters in their life who most influence how they feel and how much they suffer
- You can make their suffering in your divorce less than their current suffering if there is great conflict now between your children's parents
- You can reduce your children's suffering (& save yourself from incurring a lot of fees, trouble, and outside interference with and inspection of you and your own personal life)

Experts tell us children suffer most when their parents fight. The worst kind of fighting for children is fighting about the children. Children hate conflict. And when the conflict is about the children – the children feel responsible and horrible. So, don't fight. If you care about your children. (Unless you're fighting solely & truly to protect your children's health or safety.) Please see Potential Consequences of a Custody Dispute before you begin to fight, so you can get some idea of what may then happen.

People who fight about their children where there's no valid safety issues either ignore these plain facts – or they're ignorant of these plain facts. There's no excuse for ignoring these plain facts. And there's no excuse for being ignorant of these plain facts.

When you're a parent, you need to realize all of your actions have consequences. And, most of all, you need to realize your actions can profoundly affect your children. So think of your children first. When you do, every other decision you make becomes relatively easy. It's about your children, and what you can do to protect and nurture them; it's not just about you.

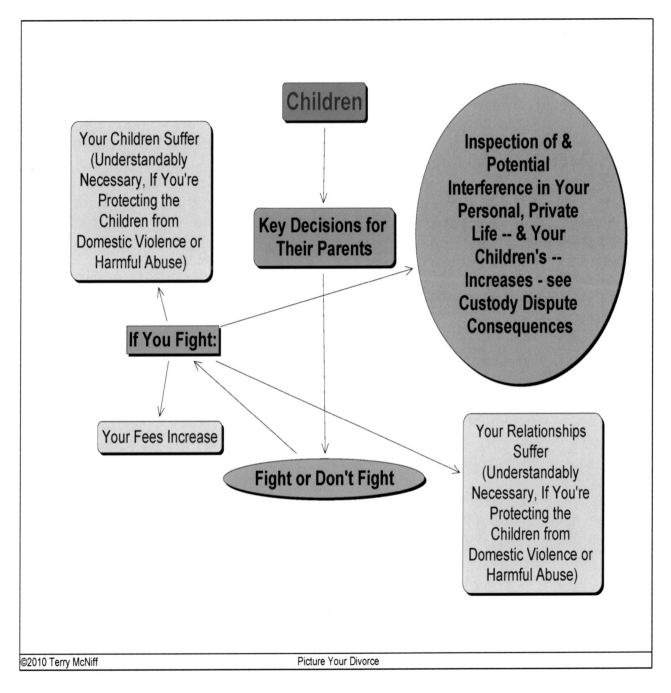

Picture Your Divorce

2. Share Your Children With Their Other Parent – Unless That Parent is Violent or Abusive.

A key decision for each divorcing custodial parent is whether to share their children. (The custodial parent or primary custodial parent is the parent who spends the majority of time caring for the children. In most relationships, 1 parent is usually the primary custodial parent.)

The answer to whether you share your children in the normal, nonviolent, non-abusive situation – is yes. Children need & want both parents. Children feel deprived when they don't get open access & contact with both parents – regardless of your feelings of the other parent.

The picture following depicts, in simple terms, what happens to your children when you don't share them with their other parent. The picture following, like all the pictures concerning children, is simple, for a reason. I don't want you to miss these simple points about how divorce affects your children. The children didn't cause the divorce. The children usually don't want the divorce. The children usually don't understand the divorce. The children usually want both parents before, during, & after divorce. It's your job to make sure they get both parents.

Sometimes, the custodial parent appears to be sharing – but puts up barriers to actual full sharing. For instance, some custodial parents impose strict requirements for the time, place, and manner of contact by the other parent. Sometimes, they're so restrictive or strict their children lose opportunities for contact with their other parent. Sometimes, the custodial parent uses their influence to convince the child not to visit – or not to have as much contact – with their other parent. Sometimes, the custodial parent uses threats, or tears, or anger, or guilt. If you're the custodial parent, you need to realize the kids generally figure out what's going on, and what you're doing to them. And, when they don't like it, they don't forget it. Ever.

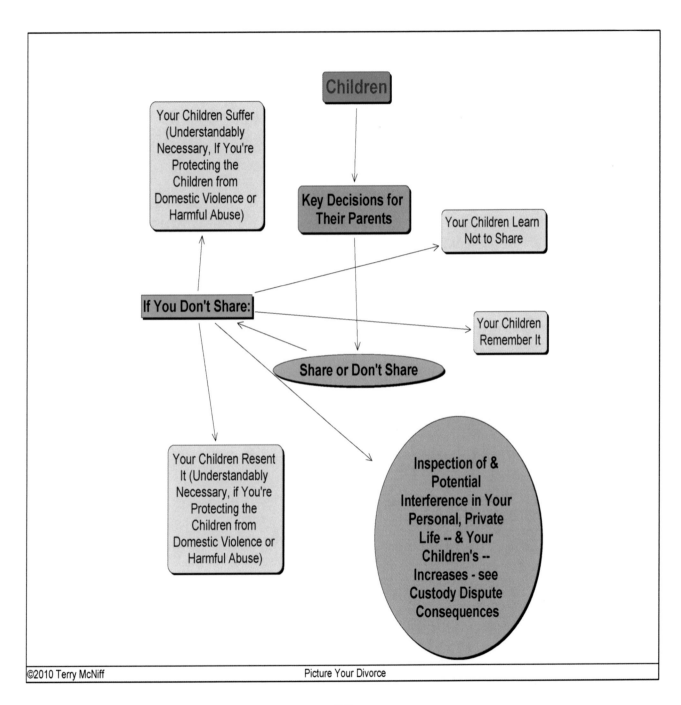

Picture Your Divorce

3. Nurture Your Children – or They'll Seek Nurturing Elsewhere.

Sometimes, divorcing parents are so wrapped up in their own anger, pain, depression or self-pity that they ignore their children. Or they fail to nurture their children. That's a big mistake.

Regardless of how much you may hurt, or just want to be left alone, or to be comforted yourself, your children need love and nurturing. Especially during divorce. When their whole world is being turned upside down. Against their wishes. For which they feel responsible. If they don't get love and nurturing from you, they'll get it somewhere else. Because they need it.

Your children might get the love and nurturing they need from:

- Their other parent

- The Internet

- That troubled kid @ school

- That other kid who seems to have little supervision or limits

- That group of kids without supervision or limits

- Somewhere – or someone – else

Nurture your children. They need it. And they deserve it. Especially during divorce.

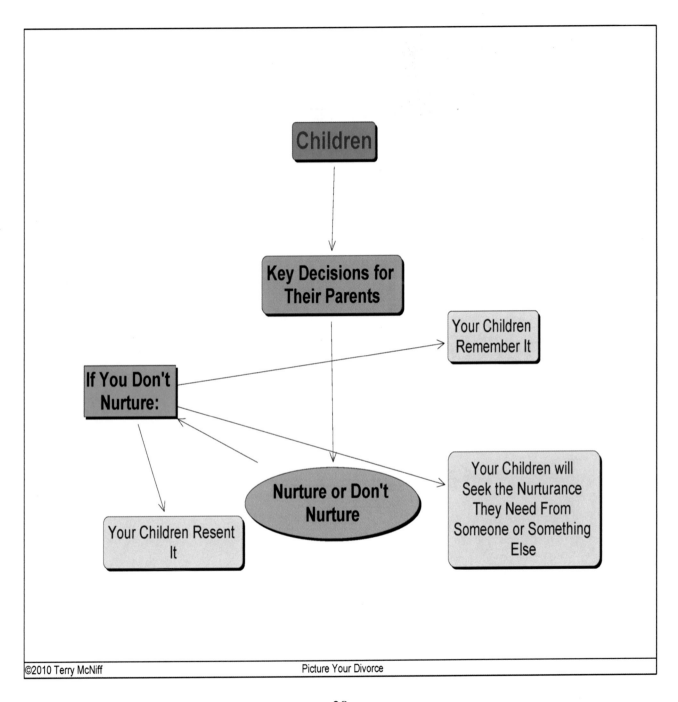

Picture Your Divorce

4. Your Children in 1 View or Picture – Don't Fight, Do Share, Do Nurture.

If you remember only 1 picture from this guide, let it be this picture.

Because this picture is the only 1 that matters to your kids.

And, if you had a crystal ball to see long into the future, you'd be able to see too – this picture is the only 1 that will matter to you.

For most of the rest of your life.

After the months or year or two your divorce takes. Even if your children have grown up and left home, they still look to their parents as role models. Will they look to you as a role model to follow – and a parent they can trust to do the right thing – or will they see you as the type of person to avoid?

In order to be remembered as most of us want to be remembered, you should study this picture carefully.

Memorize this picture.

Live this picture.

Your kids will remember.

Forever.

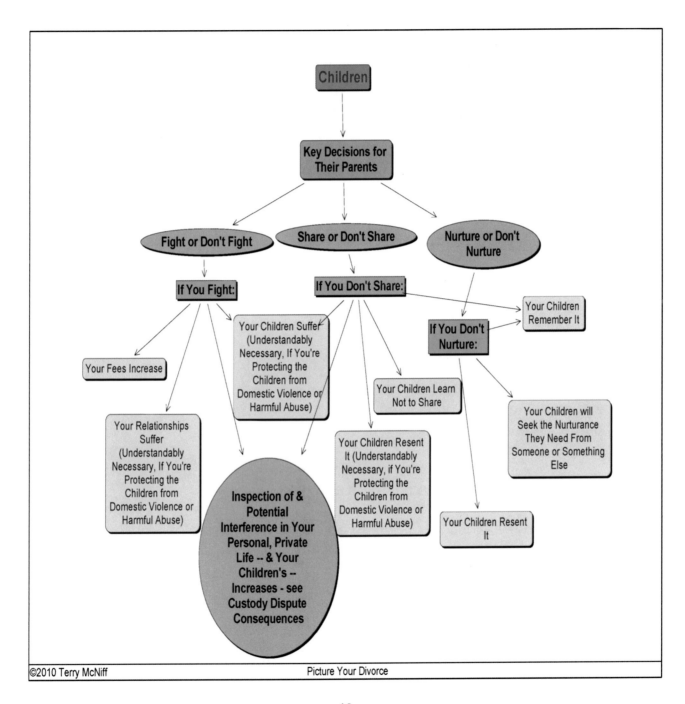

Children

Key Decisions for Their Parents

Fight or Don't Fight **Share or Don't Share** **Nurture or Don't Nurture**

If You Fight:

If You Don't Share:

If You Don't Nurture:

Your Children Remember It

Your Fees Increase

Your Children Suffer (Understandably Necessary, If You're Protecting the Children from Domestic Violence or Harmful Abuse)

Your Children Learn Not to Share

Your Relationships Suffer (Understandably Necessary, If You're Protecting the Children from Domestic Violence or Harmful Abuse)

Your Children will Seek the Nurturance They Need From Someone or Something Else

Your Children Resent It (Understandably Necessary, if You're Protecting the Children from Domestic Violence or Harmful Abuse)

Inspection of & Potential Interference in Your Personal, Private Life -- & Your Children's -- Increases - see Custody Dispute Consequences

Your Children Resent It

Picture Your Divorce

5. Some Basic Potential Consequences of a Custody Dispute Over Your Children.

For those who aren't yet convinced they can save themselves – and their children – a lot of trouble, expense, anxiety, and delay, merely by doing what's right or best for their children, I'm presenting the picture following.

This picture shows you some of the main potential consequences of your decision to fight about your children. You need to realize that once you begin to fight about your children, you have not just abdicated or abandoned your responsibility to your children.

Instead, you've also set in motion a complex series of potential events over which you have no control. First, the Court will have several options available to help the Court resolve the issues. The Court's options, include, but are not limited to all of the following:

• Appointing an attorney or attorneys for the children – even if the parents don't have their own attorneys (and you'll soon realize your children's attorneys can do almost anything they want – without much in the way of restrictions or rules or recourse, if they get it wrong)

• Imposing intrusive restrictions and psychological testing on any or all of the participants, including the parents and their children

• Appointing a Guardian ad Litem or other professional to speak for your children – and to take action on behalf of your children, against you or anyone else they feel is appropriate

• Deciding when, where and with whom your children can or can't live, go to school, be cared for, spend time with, and almost anything else the Court or the parties can dream up to fight about. You basically allow someone with different values to make decisions for your kids.

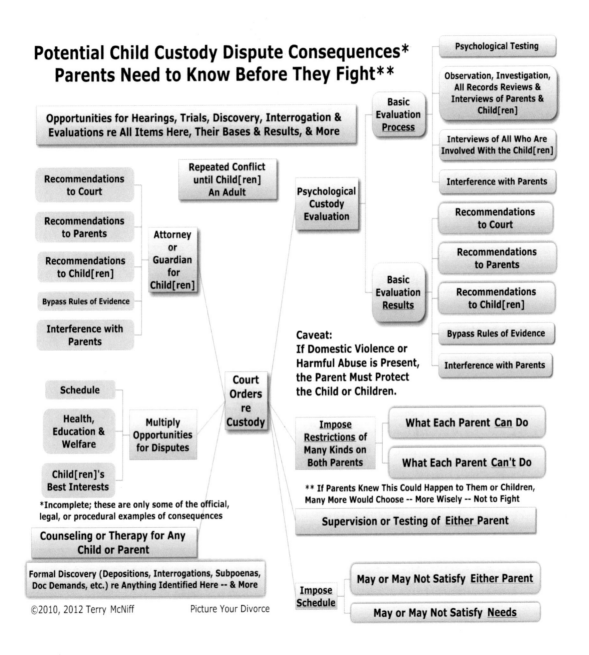

Potential Child Custody Dispute Consequences*
Parents Need to Know Before They Fight**

Psychological Testing

Observation, Investigation, All Records Reviews & Interviews of Parents & Child[ren]

Basic Evaluation Process

Opportunities for Hearings, Trials, Discovery, Interrogation & Evaluations re All Items Here, Their Bases & Results, & More

Interviews of All Who Are Involved With the Child[ren]

Interference with Parents

Recommendations to Court

Repeated Conflict until Child[ren] An Adult

Psychological Custody Evaluation

Recommendations to Court

Recommendations to Parents

Recommendations to Parents

Attorney or Guardian for Child[ren]

Recommendations to Child[ren]

Basic Evaluation Results

Recommendations to Child[ren]

Bypass Rules of Evidence

Bypass Rules of Evidence

Interference with Parents

Caveat: If Domestic Violence or Harmful Abuse is Present, the Parent Must Protect the Child or Children.

Interference with Parents

Schedule

Court Orders re Custody

Health, Education & Welfare

Multiply Opportunities for Disputes

Impose Restrictions of Many Kinds on Both Parents

What Each Parent Can Do

What Each Parent Can't Do

Child[ren]'s Best Interests

** If Parents Knew This Could Happen to Them or Children, Many More Would Choose -- More Wisely -- Not to Fight

*Incomplete; these are only some of the official, legal, or procedural examples of consequences

Supervision or Testing of Either Parent

Counseling or Therapy for Any Child or Parent

Formal Discovery (Depositions, Interrogations, Subpoenas, Doc Demands, etc.) re Anything Identified Here -- & More

May or May Not Satisfy Either Parent

Impose Schedule

May or May Not Satisfy Needs

©2010, 2012 Terry McNiff   Picture Your Divorce

D.   Dispute Resolution Methods or Processes – Choose the Right Process for You.

1.   Mediation – a Neutral Facilitator Helps You Reach Agreement.

How you choose to resolve your Divorce is critical to whether you get the best resolution at the least trouble and expense. The best way to resolve your Divorce is usually via Mediation.

Mediation is the most peaceful process. In Mediation, a trained, experienced professional works with both spouses with the goal and responsibility being to help the parties achieve a peaceful resolution. If the mediator doesn't help you reach peaceful resolution, the mediator fails. Private Mediation is usually the least stressful dispute resolution process because it is totally voluntary. (I'm not talking about mandatory mediation some states require for certain legal issues.) Either party can leave their Divorce Mediation at any time. For any reason.

Mediation starts with choosing a good Mediator. Be careful how you start to find a Mediator. If you start by telling your spouse you found a Mediator, your spouse is likely to be highly suspicious. On the other hand, if you tell your spouse you heard about a peaceful idea called Mediation that you would like your spouse to consider, most spouses will consider it.

Once your spouse has indicated he or she would like to consider Mediation, the next step is to find a suitable mediator both of you decide you like and trust. You can find a good mediator the same way you can find a good attorney. Ask around. Ask people you know who have divorced successfully. Don't hire the person with the snazziest website. That's usually a self-promoter type rather than a good mediator. Good mediators usually have first practiced family law a long time. That's right. Believe it or not, the best mediator is usually an attorney. An experienced attorney in the field usually knows the ins and outs of divorce and family law issues. They'll also usually have direct experience with what a Court can, can't, will & won't do.

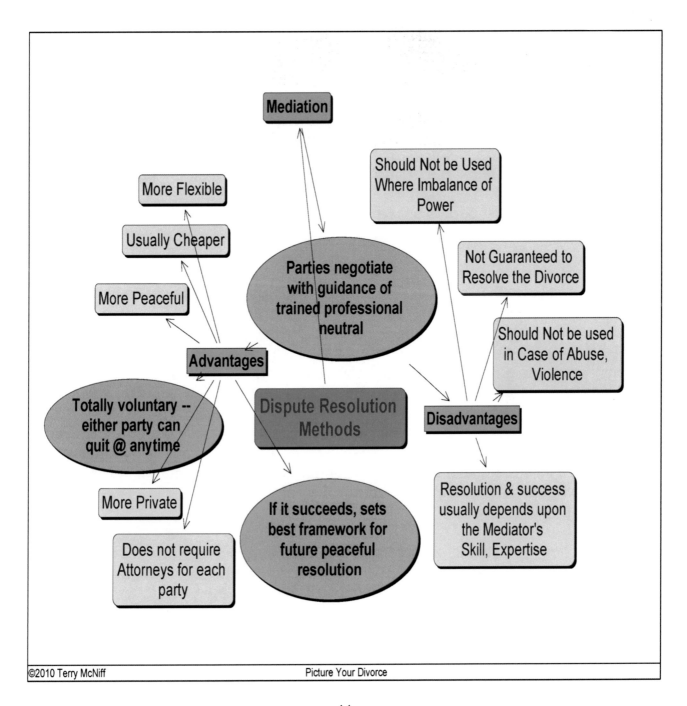

Mediation

Should Not be Used Where Imbalance of Power

More Flexible

Usually Cheaper

Parties negotiate with guidance of trained professional neutral

Not Guaranteed to Resolve the Divorce

More Peaceful

Advantages

Should Not be used in Case of Abuse, Violence

Totally voluntary -- either party can quit @ anytime

Dispute Resolution Methods

Disadvantages

More Private

Does not require Attorneys for each party

If it succeeds, sets best framework for future peaceful resolution

Resolution & success usually depends upon the Mediator's Skill, Expertise

Picture Your Divorce

2. **Negotiation** – Discussing the Issues & Exchanging Offers to Settle them.

Negotiation is another peaceful resolution process. It is harder than Mediation because:

- Most people are <u>not</u> naturally good negotiators in general

- Most people are clearly <u>not</u> good negotiators when negotiating for themselves

- Most people don't know enough about the ins and outs of divorce law to know precisely what is fair or reasonable – and often don't know how or where to start

- Most people are not able to stay level-headed or peaceful enough when trying to negotiate their own divorce – it is highly likely (almost inevitable) that at some point or points one or the other will say something the other spouse will find hurtful, or make them angry

Still, negotiation is something you will likely eventually do to resolve your divorce. A little over 90% of all cases eventually settle. And, those cases eventually settle with at least a little negotiation. Even if that negotiation is in the context of Mediation, or some other dispute resolution method. Therefore, you should study how negotiation works, & how to do it.

Then, you should picture yourself negotiating on your own behalf. If that is impossible to picture, you need to try harder. Or, just do it. If you can't do it, then get someone to help you negotiate. Because, sooner or later, you're going to want – or need – to negotiate some resolution of something. It might just be an overnight with your children. Or some sharing of something. Or some give and take involving some personal property both of you want. But, sooner or later, you'll have to do it. So the earlier you start to do it, the better it is for you.

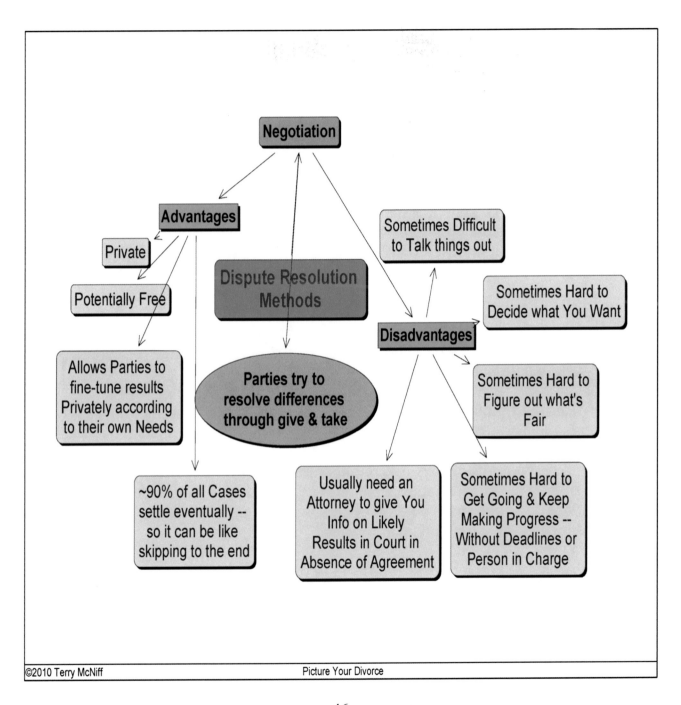

Picture Your Divorce

3. Arbitration – a Private Trial the Parties Can Create With Their Own Rules.

Arbitration is like a trial in that it involves the presentation of evidence, and the making of decisions by a neutral decision maker. Arbitration is generally a private trial – outside and away from the traditional court house and court system.

The ability to have a private resolution of any and all disputes generally appeals to most people. Despite this fact, Arbitration is rarely used by people divorcing because most divorcing people don't know about it. Another reason Arbitration is rarely used is that many divorce attorneys don't know they can use Arbitration to avoid a public trial in court.

The arbitrator most people choose is usually a retired state court judge or experienced attorney. Be careful choosing your private judge. You are empowering that judge to make life-changing decisions – without the normal recourses one has with public state court judges.

Realize that private judges, including retired state court judges, like most people, are biased. The extent of their bias may depend upon their affiliations. For instance, private judges who are part of a for-profit private judge or dispute resolution business may tend to make decisions favoring that business. The private judge business makes more money when each judge working for the business makes decisions that require the judges to spend more time on each case. So, private judging has built-in biases & problems you must recognize.

Arbitration requires the parties to decide on the rules they will apply to the decision-making process. That is also one of its major benefits. The parties can pick and choose which dispute resolution rules they will and won't use. This makes Arbitration a very flexible process some people find highly favorable or desirable. Even if they can't agree on many other things.

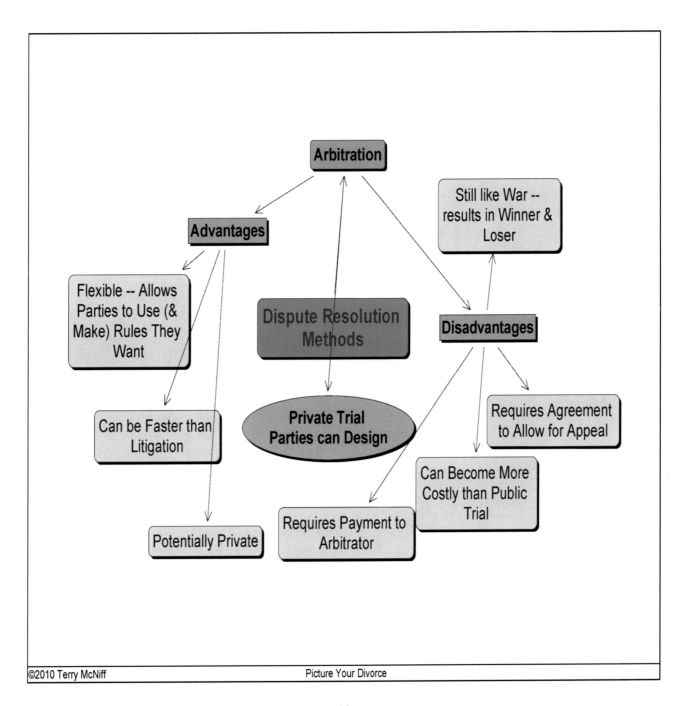

4.   <u>Collaboration</u> or Collaborative Divorce Process – Teams of Experts Work With the Parties.

Collaborative Divorce sounds like a dream. A really nice dream. Teams of professionals work together peacefully to help the parties work through their issues to reach a mutually satisfying resolution. Sounds like a dream, doesn't it?

The best part of pure Collaborative Divorce, or at least one main selling point, is that if the professionals fail to help you reach resolution, they can't be involved in the litigation that follows. That means the attorneys have a direct incentive to help you reach agreement. It's a good thing when the incentives for the attorneys correlate to your goal – reaching agreement.

But, when you analyze it, the best part of Collaborative Divorce is also the worst part. If the attorneys involved in the Collaborative Divorce can't be involved if it fails, you have to start over. Sometimes, people spend a year or more in the Collaborative Divorce process, only to find it fails. Sometimes, Collaborative Divorce is used by bullies to see if they can bully you into an unfair agreement. When they can't, they quit. The true Collaborative Divorce experts require that you start over – not just with new professionals – but also with all new evidence and analysis. One rule is you can't use anything from the Collaborative process in the litigation that follows after Collaboration fails. That means if the only evidence of fraud was uncovered in Collaboration, some say you can't use it when you have to fight to get what's fair.

Another problem with Collaborative Divorce is that many of the professionals who do it have formed a self-serving club. Whenever professionals form a club involving them working together, you should figure those professionals will look out for each other. In my experience, many collaborative professionals look out more for each other than they do for their clients. Their loyalties are divided. And, whenever loyalties are divided, that's usually bad for you.

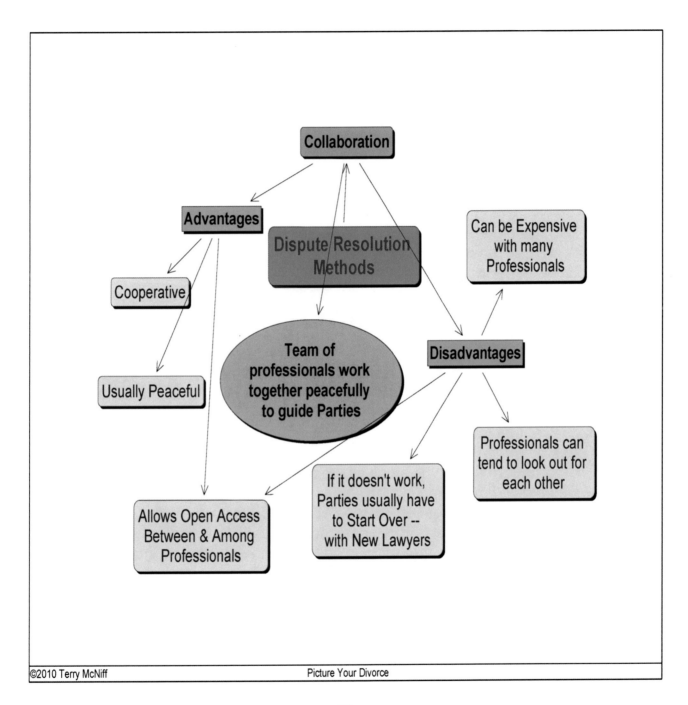

Picture Your Divorce

5. **<u>Litigation</u> – Parties Go to Court Generally in a Series of Expensive Battles.**

Litigation is the traditional court process, in all of its glory and agony. Litigation in divorce often turns into a fierce contest of perceived good versus perceived evil. It doesn't have to be that way. Neither does it have to be your first thought – or the default way of proceeding. It usually is the default, primarily because people don't know any better. Now, you know better.

For attorneys who specialize in divorce, it can become a high calling, a noble pursuit. Most of those who specialize in divorce are able to practice family law, and to litigate contested divorces, in a way that provides to each participant dignity and respect. When that happens, litigation doesn't have to be the big, ugly menace it is sometimes portrayed as in popular media.

Those who practice divorce law – but aren't specialists – usually (but not always) are at a severe disadvantage when a specialist is on the other side. Only a specialist has proven to an objective body or agency that she or he has sufficient knowledge and experience to merit a certification that many try and fail to obtain. Sometimes, they try and fail more than once.

Divorce litigation involves all of the difficult, intricate rules of procedure and evidence involved in other litigation – plus a huge body of additional legal knowledge far beyond most other litigation. Those other subjects include assets of all kinds, business, children, contracts, finances, income, liabilities, property, support – just to name a few. So, if you're engaging in litigation in your divorce, make sure you get a specialist with as much experience as you can afford. Anything less puts you at a severe disadvantage. And, in court, that can hurt. A lot. In court, either side can lose an issue in the blink of an eye – and like most things that happen when you're blinking, you won't see it. Just make sure you get an attorney who's seen enough to know it, to see it coming, and to stop it – or to make it happen. It's your choice.

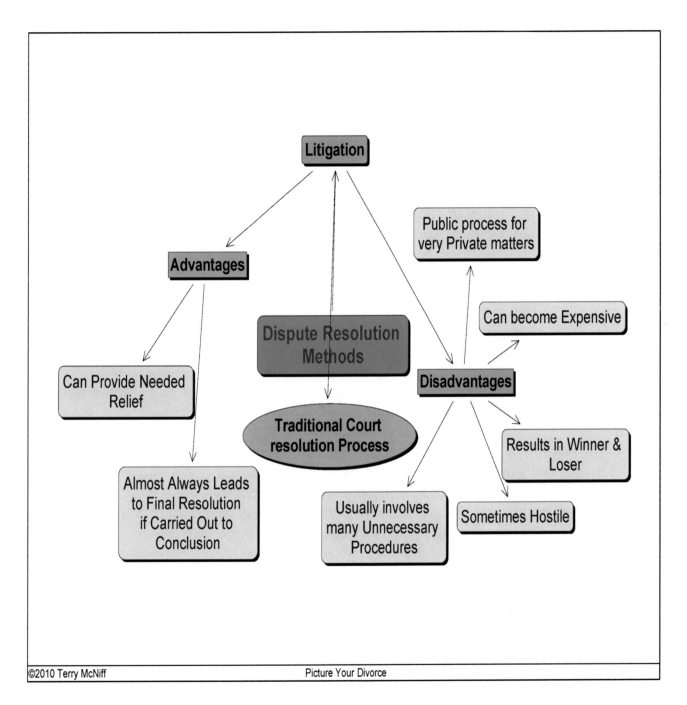

Picture Your Divorce

6. All of the normal Dispute Resolution Methods together – in 1 View to Compare & Contrast.

Please remember the picture that follows is specifically included for those who see better when they see everything together. If that's not you, and if the picture that follows looks like gibberish or looks like it has too much going on, or is too confusing, just turn the page.

Any attorney with sufficient experience and judgment can help you find the right process or method for you. You do need to be sensitive to their biases though. Attorneys who practice almost solely in litigation will be most comfortable with litigation. To those attorneys, litigation – going to court – is where people go to solve their problems.

Attorneys who are inexperienced will also be biased toward litigation. To young or inexperienced attorneys, litigation is where you can make a name for yourself. And, usually, where you can make the most money. Litigation is usually the costliest procedure. Not always. The cost, like anything else, depends upon the participants, and the experience, expertise, and effectiveness of the attorneys.

Attorneys who are members of clubs specializing in the other dispute resolution methods will similarly be biased in favor of their own club's dispute resolution methods. Now that you know that fact, and now that you know everyone has a bias, you'll know how to protect yourself against a particular bias. Be aware of it, & ask questions. (By the way, I strongly suggest you don't say you know the person you're talking to is biased. Almost every professional I know thinks he or she is not biased. And, most will resent the implication they could be biased.)

Ask the right questions to make sure whatever process or method someone is pushing is right for you. Then, pursue resolution with respect and dignity for all involved.

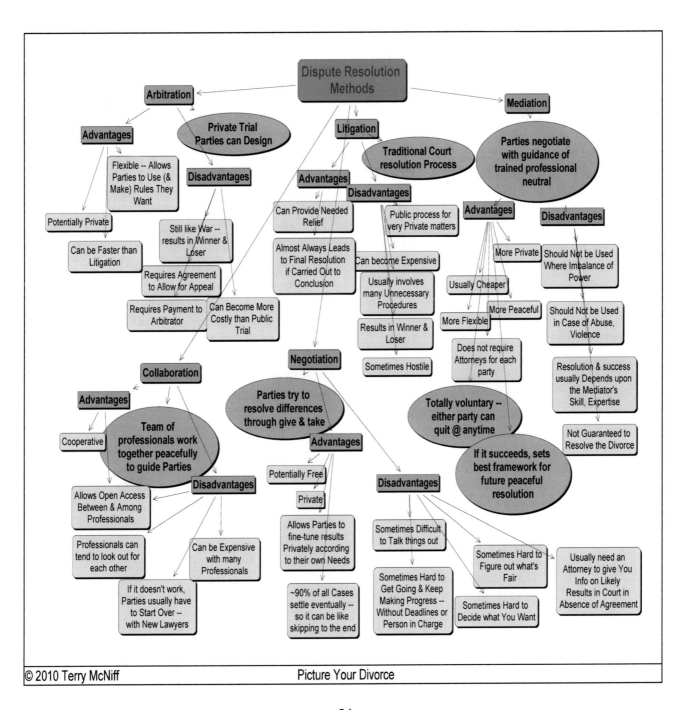

© 2010 Terry McNiff

Picture Your Divorce

54

E.   Ending Your Divorce.

1.   What is the End -- & What Does it Take to Get to the End?

Ending your Divorce earlier & better than most requires you to picture it clearly and fairly – and then make sure everything you do from that moment is directed toward that end. Sounds pretty simple, doesn't it? Many people mess it up because they fail to focus on that 1 point.

The end, for most people, is getting a Judgment or Decree of Divorce or Dissolution. In order to get that Judgment or Decree, you must complete your state's specific requirements. **Most states have 3 main required steps to get a Divorce or Dissolution:**

- **Beginning**: Filing & Serving a Petition or Complaint for Dissolution or Divorce
- **Disclosure &/or Discovery**: Parties exchange material information concerning or reflecting their assets, debts, liabilities, income, expenses, and facts related to the children
- **Ending: Judgment or Decree reached either through agreement – usually through 1 of the Dispute Resolution methods identified above – or imposed or ordered through Arbitration or Litigation**. Make sure your Judgment or Decree resolves every legal issue in the best or most complete way possible. For instance, for debts, liabilities, & obligations, specify who will pay how much to whom when, & what happens if they fail to pay – for example, they automatically forfeit something of equal or greater value, or something else you consider sufficient or equal. If you fail to specify these things for all debts & obligations, & the automatic penalties for any failures to pay or obey orders, you've required yourself to return to court to get orders to enforce the deal you thought you already had.

Your focus – and your picturing – should all be directed toward getting to a fair end. Your 3 required steps are set forth above. All you need to do to get to the end is to fill in the details to complete the required steps. Everything else is something other than getting to the end.

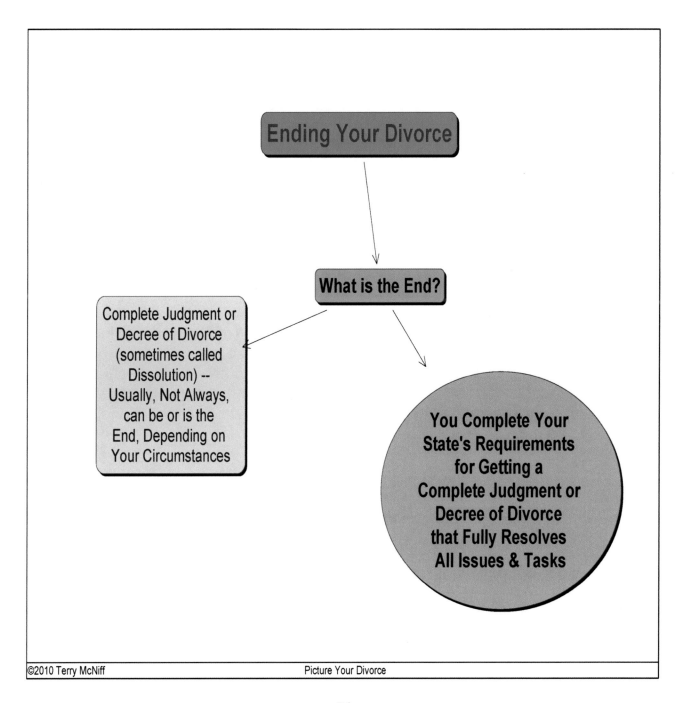

2.   How Do You Get to the End?

You get to the end faster & easier by focusing on the end – when you begin – and each moment thereafter, until you actually arrive at your destination. A final Judgment or Decree.

In order to do that, you need to **focus on learning 2 things**:

> • **What are the reasonable needs and likely entitlements of each party?**

> • **What are the reasonable and likely duties, obligations, and liabilities of each party?**

Neither of these things is usually a mystery. You can usually find some guidance that will get you into the ballpark of a reasonable resolution. You are both in the same ballpark of a reasonable resolution when you each offer a resolution that a judge would find reasonable. Once you and the other side reach the same ballpark of a reasonable resolution, when you're both making offers a judge would find reasonable, you can resolve your case peacefully.

If it becomes clear you and the other side will never (or for too long a time will not) reach the same ballpark of a reasonable resolution, you can take steps to resolve your case by the remaining dispute resolution methods available to you. Either litigation or arbitration.

For most people, there are many opportunities to take detours along the road to resolution. Most people find they can't resist the temptation to take a few detours. Sometimes, those detours are expensive, difficult, and long. Sometimes, those detours result in entirely new, longer, more expensive, and more difficult paths – veering far away from your original destination. Avoid the detours if you can.

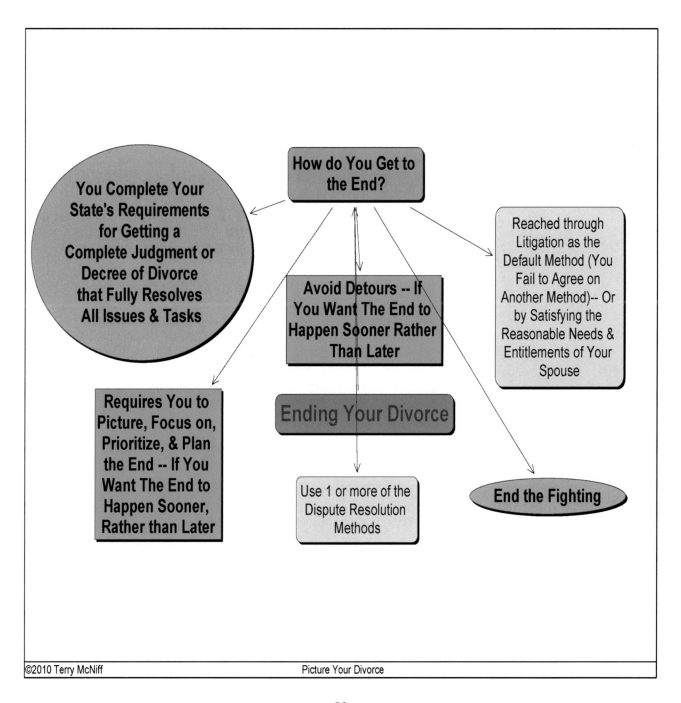

How do You Get to the End?

You Complete Your State's Requirements for Getting a Complete Judgment or Decree of Divorce that Fully Resolves All Issues & Tasks

Reached through Litigation as the Default Method (You Fail to Agree on Another Method)-- Or by Satisfying the Reasonable Needs & Entitlements of Your Spouse

Avoid Detours -- If You Want The End to Happen Sooner Rather Than Later

Ending Your Divorce

Requires You to Picture, Focus on, Prioritize, & Plan the End -- If You Want The End to Happen Sooner, Rather than Later

Use 1 or more of the Dispute Resolution Methods

End the Fighting

Picture Your Divorce

58

3. What are the Main Detours to Avoid on Your Way to the End of Your Divorce?

Most of the main detours consist of **<u>unnecessary disputes</u>** in your divorce. For instance, you can get bogged down in or diverted by unnecessary disputes concerning:

- child custody or visitation issues,
- child support issues,
- alimony or spousal support issues,
- property control or use issues, keeping in mind property includes debts, liabilities, and obligations, and who is required to pay what to whom when with what penalties for any failures,
- issues concerning interim relief (relief pending final trial or final resolution concerning any issues you or your spouse may want to fight about – or need to resolve),
- failures or refusals to provide discovery or information to your spouse, and
- issues concerning the exact nature, extent and language of court orders the court may or may not have made concerning any or all issues.

Looking at the simple picture following concerning these potential disputes, you'll see that at no time do any of the disputes lead back to the divorce resolution track or road. That's because these disputes are detours. They're different from public road detours in that there are no clear signs in divorce detours to get you back on track to your destination. And no clear end. Divorce detours don't end until both of you decide to get to the end – and get back on the road you want to travel on to your destination – or the Court imposes an end to the dispute.

You should remember how divorce detours work when it comes time for you to decide how you want to resolve issues in your divorce. If you choose a method other than agreement, you may get sidetracked on a detour of unknown duration. At an unknown cost or costs. Possibly for unknown or unlikely benefits.

Divorce Dispute Detours

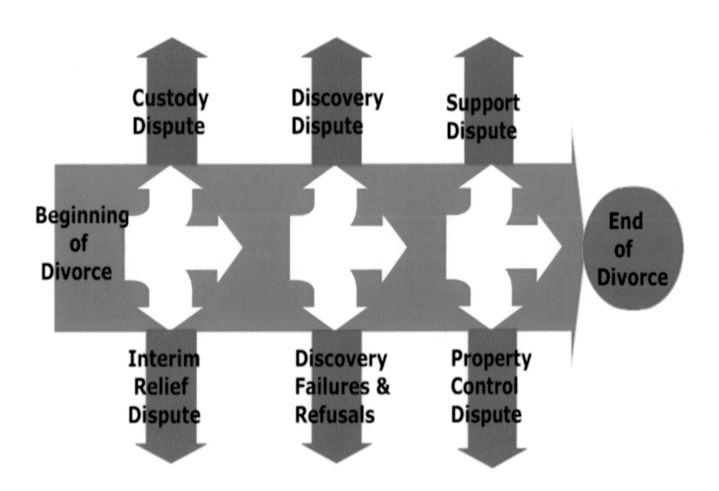

Picture Your Divorce

60

4. When is a Detour not just a Detour? When It turns into a Vicious Cycle of Conflict.

I get the distinct impression many people feel they can beat the odds – and take a very short detour down the conflict path – and then return almost immediately from the short conflict path back to the dispute resolution path. This kind of thinking is generally wrong.

These people don't understand the dynamics of conflict. When you make a personal attack against your spouse, your spouse feels irresistibly drawn to retaliate. You can wish that weren't so. You can feel like you know your spouse well enough to know your spouse won't do that. To you. Or to themselves. But, generally speaking, in my experience, you'll be mistaken.

You generally don't know what a cornered person will do – until that person feels cornered. The dynamic of conflict tending to lead to more conflict is multiplied by other factors:

- Generally, when you attack your spouse in the divorce context, your attack is public – usually a public record available to everyone for the asking.

- Most people attacked publicly will feel a stronger desire to retaliate – in a stronger fashion – to prove to the world they're not the bad guy.

- Most attacks in the divorce context tend to be more personal than in any other context – usually attacking the entire person on a direct personal level.

- Most people consider their private life to be their own personal refuge or sacred peaceful place – and when you disturb or destroy that refuge – it upsets them a lot, and tends to make them act less rationally, sometimes viciously or fiercely.

Vicious Cycle of Conflict

© 2010 Terry McNiff　　　Picture Your Divorce

5. When is the End not The End? When You or Your Ex Make it That Way.

A Judgment or Decree of Divorce or Dissolution is not the complete end when you or your Ex left something out – or when there is something that must be resolved later.

It's much better for you if you can end the Divorce 1 time. And make that 1 end be the end of everything – including all or most of the opportunities to fight again later.

The best way to only have to go through your Divorce once is to picture all that could come up in the future – and deal with all of those things fairly in your Judgment or Decree. Specify all that must be done, who is doing it, how & when, & what happens if they don't do it.

If your children are young when you divorce, then consider what changes you or your Ex might want to make to custody, visitation, or child support as your children mature. You can provide for all of the likely changes or modifications in your original Judgment or Decree.

If you have pension plans, resist the urge to just reserve jurisdiction to have the court resolve the division later. There are many ways to resolve it now. And, it's not that hard.

If you had a long-term marriage, and you may have long-term spousal support or alimony, you can decide now how to deal with that issue in stages, until termination.

If you have some property that is hard to agree on, review the picture showing how to divide property. (Please see section P. Property Division, below.) There are many ways to figure out how to divide the property now – even if it's hard for you and your spouse to agree. You're usually far better off dividing all property now – rather than later – for many reasons.

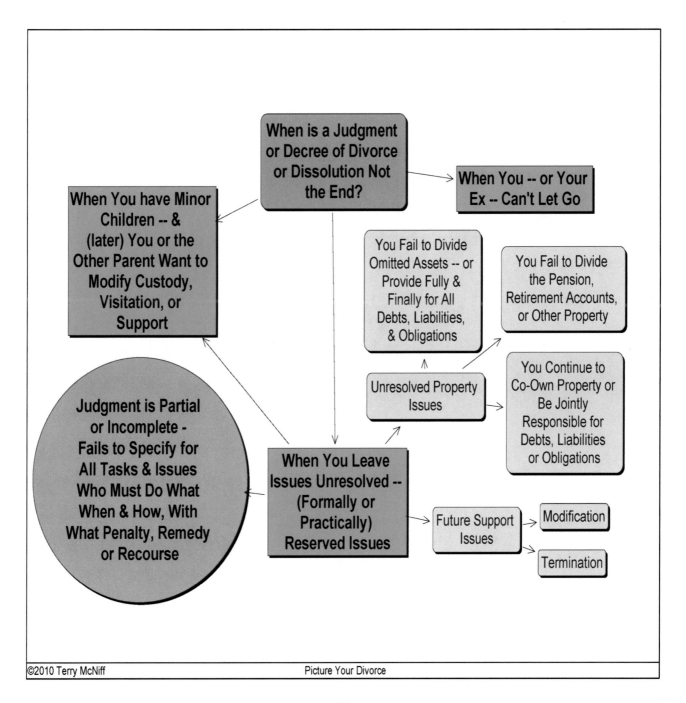

When is a Judgment or Decree of Divorce or Dissolution Not the End?

When You -- or Your Ex -- Can't Let Go

When You have Minor Children -- & (later) You or the Other Parent Want to Modify Custody, Visitation, or Support

You Fail to Divide Omitted Assets -- or Provide Fully & Finally for All Debts, Liabilities, & Obligations

You Fail to Divide the Pension, Retirement Accounts, or Other Property

Unresolved Property Issues

You Continue to Co-Own Property or Be Jointly Responsible for Debts, Liabilities or Obligations

Judgment is Partial or Incomplete - Fails to Specify for All Tasks & Issues Who Must Do What When & How, With What Penalty, Remedy or Recourse

When You Leave Issues Unresolved -- (Formally or Practically) Reserved Issues

Future Support Issues

Modification

Termination

Picture Your Divorce

6. Ending Your Divorce – Putting it All Together.

Resolution is possible at any – and every stage – of your Divorce. For instance, you and your spouse could agree to all issues in your divorce before either one of you files anything in Court. Or, you can take months or years, and wait until a full-blown court trial. Or have several trials. Or fight endlessly. The choice is yours.

Many people make the mistake of trying to get a perfect resolution. Done is usually far better than perfect. And, perfect usually only comes in fairy tales – or movies.

Brainstorm, and then analyze:

- What is it precisely that you need from your Divorce?

- Is it reasonable to expect that you can get it?

- What do you think the other side wants or needs?

- Is it reasonable to expect that the other side can get what they want or need?

- If so, is there any reason you don't give them what they want or need? In return for what you reasonably want & need?

- Are your reasons something other than anger, jealousy, or selfishness?

- If not, give it up. Get it done.

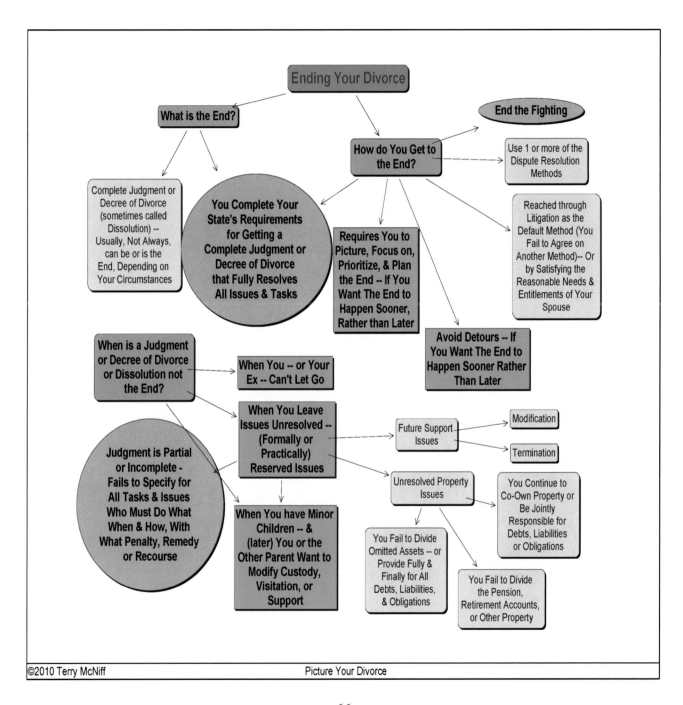

Ending Your Divorce

What is the End?

End the Fighting

How do You Get to the End?

Use 1 or more of the Dispute Resolution Methods

Complete Judgment or Decree of Divorce (sometimes called Dissolution) -- Usually, Not Always, can be or is the End, Depending on Your Circumstances

You Complete Your State's Requirements for Getting a Complete Judgment or Decree of Divorce that Fully Resolves All Issues & Tasks

Requires You to Picture, Focus on, Prioritize, & Plan the End -- If You Want The End to Happen Sooner, Rather than Later

Reached through Litigation as the Default Method (You Fail to Agree on Another Method)-- Or by Satisfying the Reasonable Needs & Entitlements of Your Spouse

Avoid Detours -- If You Want The End to Happen Sooner Rather Than Later

When is a Judgment or Decree of Divorce or Dissolution not the End?

When You -- or Your Ex -- Can't Let Go

When You Leave Issues Unresolved -- (Formally or Practically) Reserved Issues

Future Support Issues

Modification

Termination

Judgment is Partial or Incomplete - Fails to Specify for All Tasks & Issues Who Must Do What When & How, With What Penalty, Remedy or Recourse

Unresolved Property Issues

You Continue to Co-Own Property or Be Jointly Responsible for Debts, Liabilities or Obligations

When You have Minor Children -- & (later) You or the Other Parent Want to Modify Custody, Visitation, or Support

You Fail to Divide Omitted Assets -- or Provide Fully & Finally for All Debts, Liabilities, & Obligations

You Fail to Divide the Pension, Retirement Accounts, or Other Property

Picture Your Divorce

66

F.   Finances & $.

1.   If You Depend Upon Your Spouse for Support or $, Consider **All** Your Options.

For some people, it's all about the money. Of course, most of us need some money to survive. So, money is clearly important. If you have children & need money to support them, money is critical.

But, I believe the money issue is relatively simple.[2] And, simpler than many people make it. You either have it or you don't. If you don't have it, the question is where you can get it. If you have no source other than your spouse, and your spouse has much more, then your spouse is usually going to have to pay something. The question then becomes how do you get it, and how much do you get?

The question of how much is usually where the dispute lies. The supported or receiving spouse thinks the paying spouse needs to pay as much as before the 2 sides split into 2 households to support. The supporting spouse thinks the other side demands too much.

Fortunately, for most people in most states there are guidelines for how much is the right amount. Those guidelines cover most cases. So, if the other side is requesting the guideline amount, or pretty close to it, you should agree to it. (Please see section S. Support for more guidance on support.)

For those who can't agree, if you're stuck on being unable to accept 1 penny different than you feel you deserve, you need to realize you will often have to pay extra for your unwillingness to reach a reasonable agreement.

---

[2] Recognizing I could be making the money issue too simple for some people, & for some cases, I left more extra space than usual in the picture following, and I have dealt with money issues in many pictures and sections. Remember the pictures in this book are merely guides for your use to draw your own pictures to suit your purposes and needs. Also, for guidance on the particular rules and factors concerning money, please refer to the section dealing with the particular money issues you're concerned about, for instance, section P. Property Division, or section S. Support.

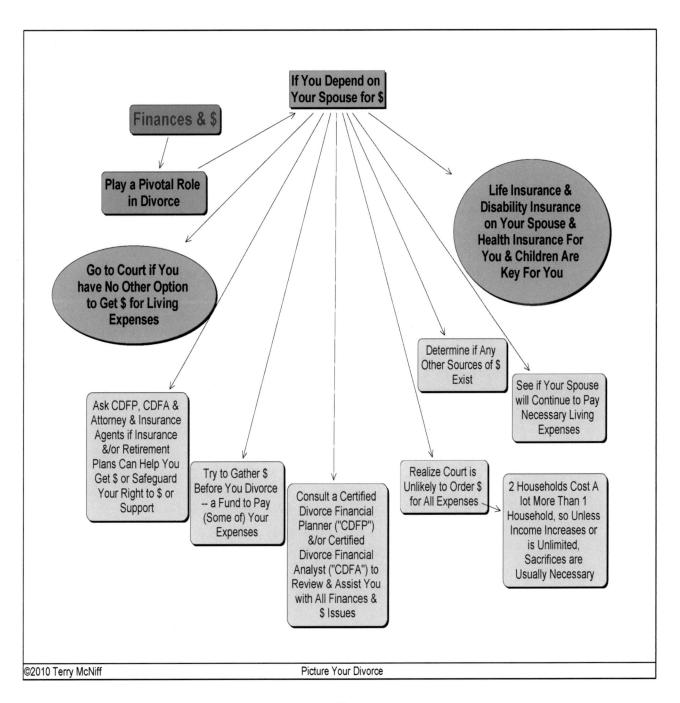

Picture Your Divorce

2. If You're the Supporting Spouse, Be Careful – It's Not Good if You Fight.

Right about now, some people seeing the picture following are jumping for joy over 1 idea:

Cutting off your spouse makes your spouse angry

You people jumping: Quit jumping for joy! You don't want to make your spouse angry.

Almost everyone I've observed take joy in making their spouse angry has lived to regret it.

Don't be 1 of those people who intentionally makes their spouse angry, and takes joy in it.

If you do, you'll regret it too.

If you make your spouse angry enough – or desperate enough – to go to court to fight (perhaps viciously in retaliation – or merely from a feeling of a need to fight to survive):

- Your fees will increase, costing you more money;
- Your spouse's fees will increase, usually costing you more money;
- The court might determine you owe more than you thought was reasonable, costing you more money;
- You could very easily be on your way to creating a significant detour away from final resolution, or away from the end, likely costing you more money, time, uncertainty, and anxiety; and
- If you have children, your children are likely to find out what you did, and they won't likely forget it.

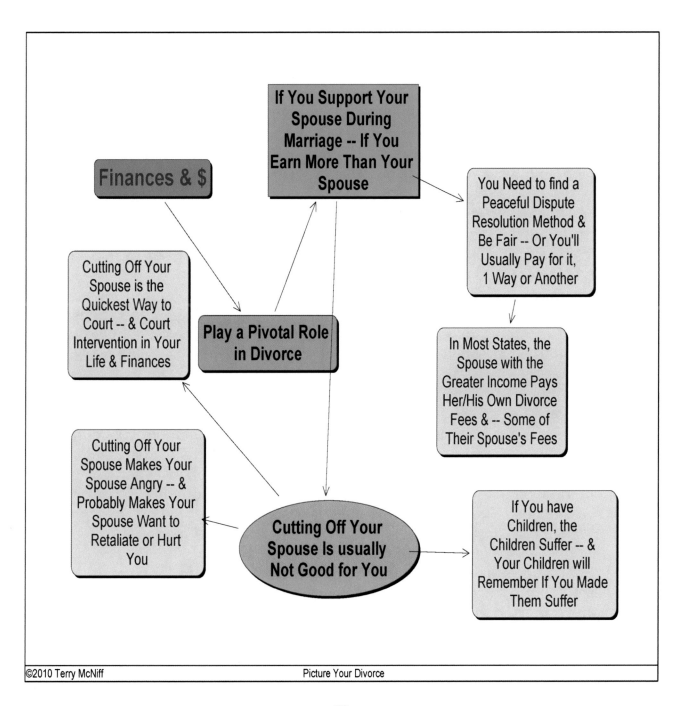

Finances & $

If You Support Your Spouse During Marriage -- If You Earn More Than Your Spouse

You Need to find a Peaceful Dispute Resolution Method & Be Fair -- Or You'll Usually Pay for it, 1 Way or Another

Cutting Off Your Spouse is the Quickest Way to Court -- & Court Intervention in Your Life & Finances

Play a Pivotal Role in Divorce

In Most States, the Spouse with the Greater Income Pays Her/His Own Divorce Fees & -- Some of Their Spouse's Fees

Cutting Off Your Spouse Makes Your Spouse Angry -- & Probably Makes Your Spouse Want to Retaliate or Hurt You

Cutting Off Your Spouse Is usually Not Good for You

If You have Children, the Children Suffer -- & Your Children will Remember If You Made Them Suffer

Picture Your Divorce

3. Finances & $ -- Each Spouse has Choices & There's (Often) Only 1 Pie.

Sometimes, spouses in a divorce forget the other spouse has choices. That's a key point to remember. Whenever a spouse thinks they have painted the other spouse into a corner, they sometimes feel like they're in control, and have the other spouse right where they want them.

That feeling is usually a mistake. The spouse who has that mistaken feeling seems to need to be brought to the sometimes painful realization that the other spouse has choices. The other spouse can choose a path into the court venue. That costs everybody time and money.

The other spouse also has other options. For instance, if the spouse with the money & income cuts off the other spouse or makes money too tight for the other spouse, the other spouse can potentially move away with the children. That usually hurts a lot.

Some courts have restrictions on moving with the children. But, usually the restrictions are in place to make sure a move is not made for the sole purpose of cutting off the other parent's contact with the children. That's a difficult thing to prove. The point to keep in mind is that the other spouse has options when you squeeze them or cut them off. Moving away is just one of the potential options, depending upon your circumstances. The other spouse may have various other options available to her or him to even the scales – or even the score – or just to get revenge.

The spouse who is dependent upon the other spouse for support needs to realize that the income pie does not get bigger when the other spouse leaves. The income that used to support 1 household now needs to support 2 households – and that will require some often painful adjustments. The pie does not automatically get bigger by going to court. That costs money.

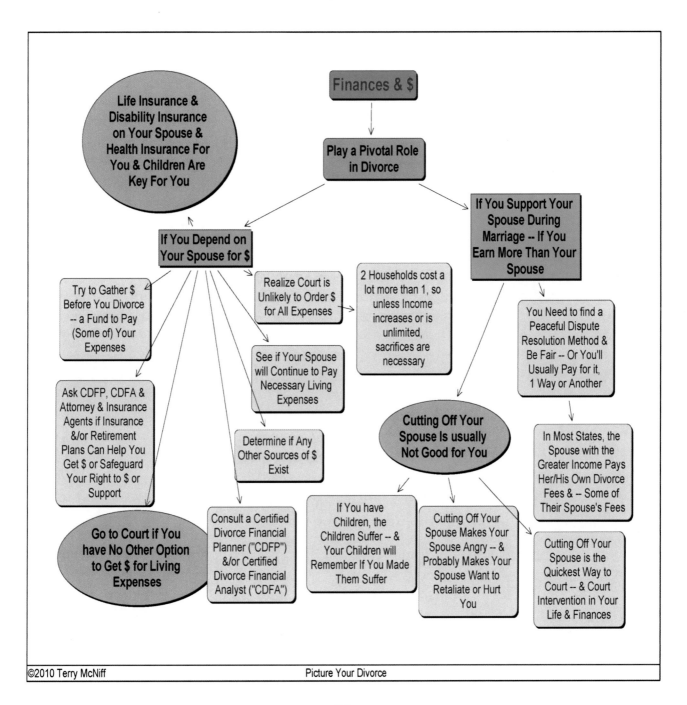

Finances & $

Play a Pivotal Role in Divorce

Life Insurance & Disability Insurance on Your Spouse & Health Insurance For You & Children Are Key For You

If You Depend on Your Spouse for $

If You Support Your Spouse During Marriage -- If You Earn More Than Your Spouse

Try to Gather $ Before You Divorce -- a Fund to Pay (Some of) Your Expenses

Realize Court is Unlikely to Order $ for All Expenses

2 Households cost a lot more than 1, so unless Income increases or is unlimited, sacrifices are necessary

You Need to find a Peaceful Dispute Resolution Method & Be Fair -- Or You'll Usually Pay for it, 1 Way or Another

Ask CDFP, CDFA & Attorney & Insurance Agents if Insurance &/or Retirement Plans Can Help You Get $ or Safeguard Your Right to $ or Support

See if Your Spouse will Continue to Pay Necessary Living Expenses

Determine if Any Other Sources of $ Exist

Cutting Off Your Spouse Is usually Not Good for You

In Most States, the Spouse with the Greater Income Pays Her/His Own Divorce Fees & -- Some of Their Spouse's Fees

Go to Court if You have No Other Option to Get $ for Living Expenses

Consult a Certified Divorce Financial Planner ("CDFP") &/or Certified Divorce Financial Analyst ("CDFA")

If You have Children, the Children Suffer -- & Your Children will Remember If You Made Them Suffer

Cutting Off Your Spouse Makes Your Spouse Angry -- & Probably Makes Your Spouse Want to Retaliate or Hurt You

Cutting Off Your Spouse is the Quickest Way to Court -- & Court Intervention in Your Life & Finances

Picture Your Divorce

G.   Goals & Priorities that are Reasonable Will Help You Make Better Divorce Decisions.

Goals & priorities are the key to resolving your divorce successfully.

With goals, you know where you want to go. Without goals, you don't know where you want to go. Without goals, it's like you're driving around without any destination, without knowing anything: where you're going, when you've arrived, and when your trip is over.

If you have multiple goals, then you need to analyze and prioritize. Which goal is the most important to you? Which goal is second most important to you? Which goal is third most important to you? And so on. Once you've done that, everything else – including your decisions – should fall into place. As long as you're being consistent. And analyzing correctly.

Your #1 goal might be to spare the children from conflict.

Your #1 goal might be to get every penny you can. Or to be fair.

Your #1 goal might be to keep the house. Or sell it. Or give it to your spouse.

Your #1 goal may be any number of things, depending on your personal situation.

As long as your #1 goal is reasonable, you should be able to evaluate what you need to do about everything that comes up, whether you planned for it, or not. It helps to plan, of course. It helps to study the options. And it helps to picture what's most likely to come up. But, even if you didn't plan for something to come up, if you have a reasonable goal or goals, you'll usually know what you should do.

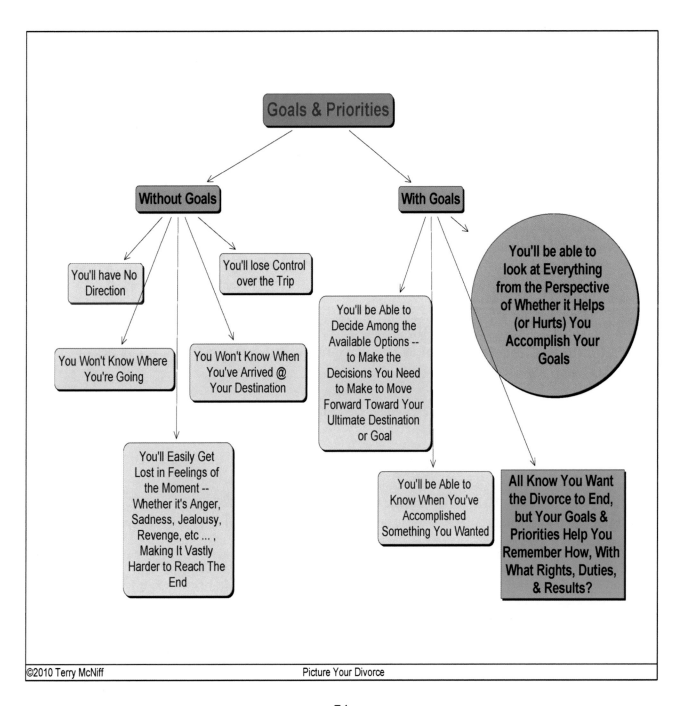

Picture Your Divorce

H.   Health Under Stress.

You should take affirmative steps to protect and strengthen your health while experiencing your divorce. You need to be healthy to make your best decisions under divorce stress.

Only those who have endured a painful divorce understand the difficulty of going through a divorce. The stress of a divorce itself makes decision-making extremely difficult. If you don't find a way to deal with such stress that is effective for you, your decision-making – and your health – deteriorates. That can result in a downward spiral.

Those who want to go through their divorce as successfully as possible – and to avoid a downward spiral – need to recognize divorce is one of the most stressful things you can go through. As the psychologists tell us, the first step to dealing with any problem is to recognize it is a problem. Also recognize the connections between health and decision-making.

1.   The 5 Stages of Grief.

The psychologists also tell us that in a divorce each party usually goes through the 5 stages of grief. Not everyone goes through the 5 stages of grief in the same way. So your experience will still – and always – be personal to you. But, you can learn the 5 stages of grief, their likelihood, and what you can do to get through them in healthy, positive ways.

Thanks to the Internet, the nuts and bolts of this type of information are all over the place. You just need to make sure you're reviewing the information from a reliable source. That proves true for everything you look for on the Internet. The best websites usually end in .gov, .edu, or .org. And, usually, they have a long history of helping people – without profit or ads.

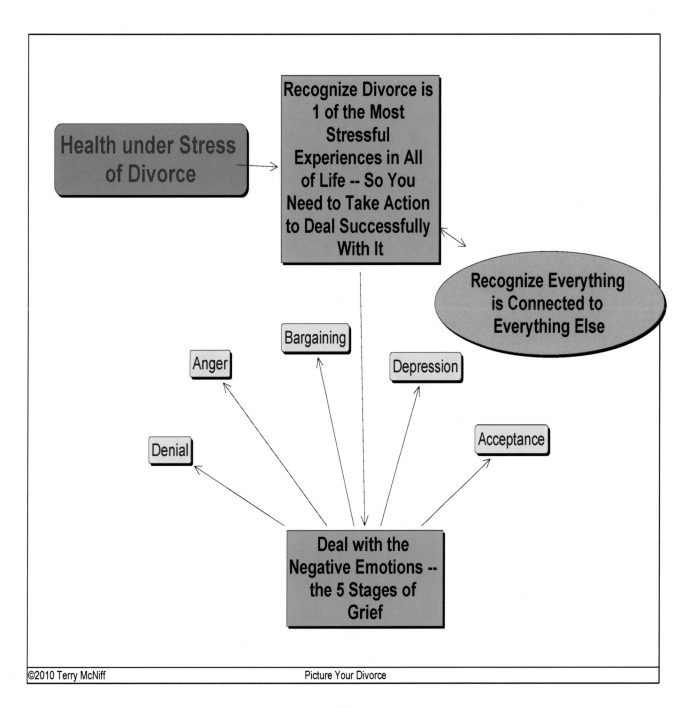

Picture Your Divorce

2. Health has Many Components, Each of Which Requires Your Attention.

One side of the health equation is the negative side, or the absence of illness, injuries, or impairments that might prevent you from living a healthy life to the best of your ability. I realize it is difficult – and not altogether beneficial – to look at only the negative side of health.

Realize everything is connected to everything else. You usually can't be completely healthy without dealing with your health on both the negative side, dealing with illness, and the positive side, dealing with good things to do to make yourself stronger and healthier.

But, we have to start somewhere to break health down into its essential elements. And the negative side is a good place to start. For several reasons. First of all, most people view divorce as a huge negative. Tell someone you're going through a divorce – and watch their reaction. It's almost like you have a fatal disease. Or a real bad contagious disease. You can usually see or sense an immediate pullback. A sense of revulsion. Or repulsion.

Another reason to look at the negative side first is that people often get lost in the negative side. Negativity can pull you down – not like gravity pulls you down, but stronger. With gravity, it's easy to get up – just use your muscles. It's not easy to get up from the negativity of divorce.

But you need to get up, and you can get up – with a healthy outlook, and a bit of determination. If you look at all the components of health, and work on them all, you'll get healthier. If you are not healthy in one or more components of health – it will affect the other components of health. Almost always negatively. Not always immediately. But eventually – like a slow-spreading cancer. And, nobody wants a cancer. So, get going. On to the positive side.

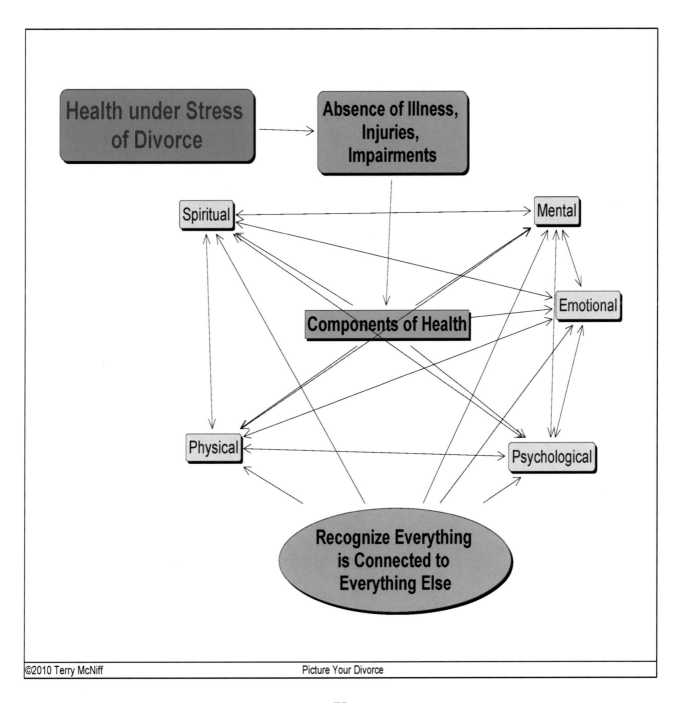

Picture Your Divorce

78

3. Getting Healthy – on the Positive Side – Despite the Stress.

The good news is: Everyone can usually get healthy – or at least, healthier – despite the stress of divorce. Many have done it. The main questions is: Are you going to be 1 of those people who has a good divorce? Or a bad divorce?

Surprisingly, the answer is often up to you. Even though it doesn't always seem that way. Almost 1/2 of us feel like victims first. If you're one of those people, you might choose to wallow in self-pity. But, self-pity won't solve any of your problems. And, while you're wallowing in self-pity, life goes on. Stuff happens. And, you need to deal with a lot of the stuff that goes on in your own life. The best way to do that well is to develop a healthy attitude

Attitude makes a huge difference. In everything. So, how do you develop a healthy attitude?

A healthy attitude comes primarily from 3 things:

- Determine – consciously decide & set as a goal – that you will become healthy

- Pursue -- & appreciate – humor (as laughing is very health-inducing)

- Find Refuge – something good for you that you enjoy – and pursue it regularly

Do those 3 things, everyday, and you'll find health. Much sooner than most. Much better than most. It's really that simple. Try it yourself.

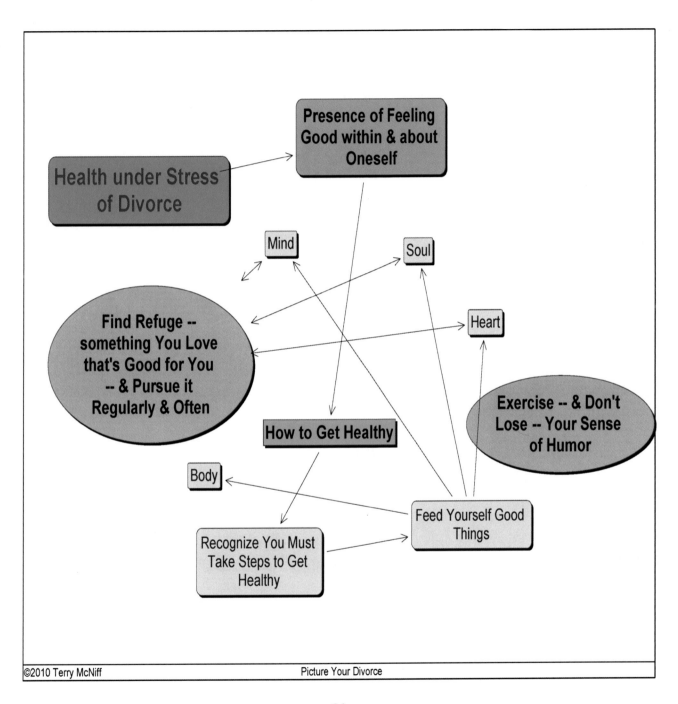

Picture Your Divorce

4.   Getting Healthy – Putting It All Together.

To me, the picture following says it all. And, to those who want or need to see the whole thing together, the picture following is a thing of beauty. It's all there.

If you're not one of those people who wants or needs to see it all – and especially if you're one of those people who can be overwhelmed by a comprehensive picture like this, close your eyes and turn the page. When you're ready to work on getting healthy, use the earlier pictures and just take it 1 step at a time.

One thing to keep in mind about getting – and staying – healthy under stress is that your progress is not always forward. Progress – under adversity – does not come in a straight line.

You might sometimes find yourself taking the proverbial one to two steps forward – and one or two steps back. But, if you persist trying to move forward, you'll get there. Despite the setbacks.

When we're talking about getting healthy, the old axiom is true – slow and steady wins this race. Health comes to those who keep after it. And after it. Just don't give up.

You can – and will – have moments of doubt. And anger at your ex. And anger at yourself. And disappointment. And regret. And other negative feelings.

But the key thing to remember is that divorce is rarely fatal. Many other people have gone through divorce and survived. You can too. And you'll make it a lot easier on yourself if you develop a picture and a plan.

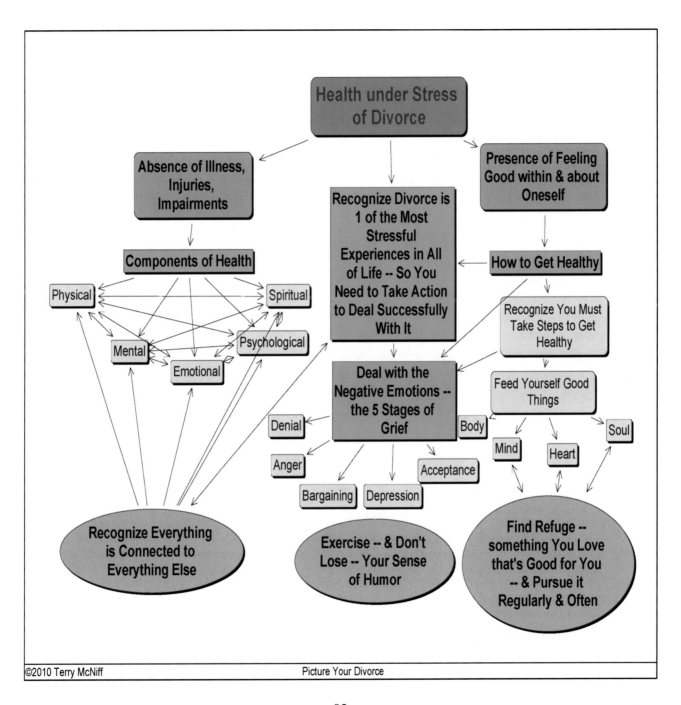

Picture Your Divorce

82

I. Information is Critical to Resolving Your Divorce Finally & Fairly.

1. You Can Give Information Willingly -- & Save Yourself Time, Money & Trouble.

In each divorce, one spouse often has possession or control of all or most of the critical information. For instance, in many marriages, one spouse primarily manages the parties' financial information and affairs. In a divorce, the other party, the non-managing party, is going to need access to financial information in order to reach a fair resolution of the financial issues.

For some reason, this simple truth is lost on many spouses who possess or control most of the critical financial information. For some reason, many spouses still think they can successfully hide pertinent financial information – and keep it away from the other side. In most states, discovery and disclosure of material financial information are mandatory. That means you're required to disclose to your spouse everything material. And, in many states, failure to provide discovery and disclosure to the other side can lead to severe penalties against the failing party, including money damages, fees, and forfeiture of property.

So, what is material information that you're probably required to disclose to your spouse? You can think of material information in at least 2 ways. First, you can consider material information to be the information you can picture a judge saying is information you should have disclosed. Second, you can consider material information to include any information you would want to know if your roles were reversed, and your spouse had the information, or knew about it, and you didn't have it or didn't know about it. If you look at it that way, it's easy to figure it out.

You have the choice to disclose all material information to your spouse willingly. If you do, you'll save yourself time, money, and trouble. The choice is up to you.

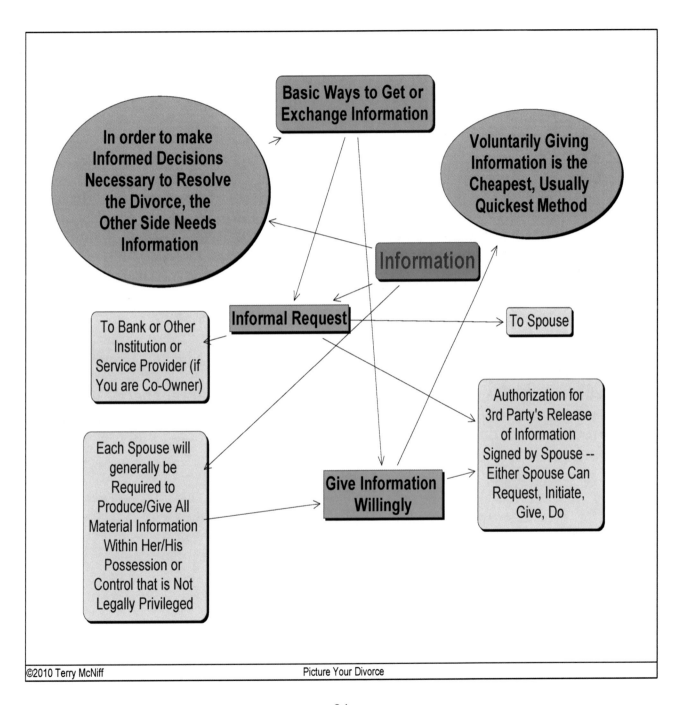

Basic Ways to Get or Exchange Information

In order to make Informed Decisions Necessary to Resolve the Divorce, the Other Side Needs Information

Voluntarily Giving Information is the Cheapest, Usually Quickest Method

Information

Informal Request

To Spouse

To Bank or Other Institution or Service Provider (if You are Co-Owner)

Authorization for 3rd Party's Release of Information Signed by Spouse -- Either Spouse Can Request, Initiate, Give, Do

Each Spouse will generally be Required to Produce/Give All Material Information Within Her/His Possession or Control that is Not Legally Privileged

Give Information Willingly

Picture Your Divorce

2. You Can <u>Refuse</u> to Give Information Willingly – & Fight & Object – But It'll Cost You.

If you don't give all of the material information to your spouse willingly, you need to realize that's not the end of it. Your spouse has options too. The Court also has options.

Your spouse can use many formal methods to obtain information from you and others. The picture following shows many of the formal methods used to obtain disclosure or discovery. You should look at most of those methods to obtain information as easy and cheap to request. And, you should also look at those methods as expensive and difficult to respond to – because most of the responses are required to be under oath – after you have conducted a diligent search and inquiry. And, if you mess up under oath – there can be severe, costly consequences.

In many states, the duty to disclose pertinent financial information has been transformed into an affirmative duty. In traditional litigation, including divorce litigation back in the 1990's and before, each party only had to answer specific questions or provide specifically, properly requested information. If the other side failed to ask correctly, they didn't get the information. And, the responding party did not have the affirmative duty to provide it.

Those days where parties could play such games are long past in many states. (Make sure you know whether your divorce is in a state that allows game-playing and withholding of pertinent information or not. You can pay a much higher price in some states.) However, even if you are in game-playing or withholding state, you need to know that most states allow judgments and orders to be cancelled or set aside on the basis of fraud, which can include non-disclosure. Is that a risk you want to take? Do you really want to have to do it all over again?

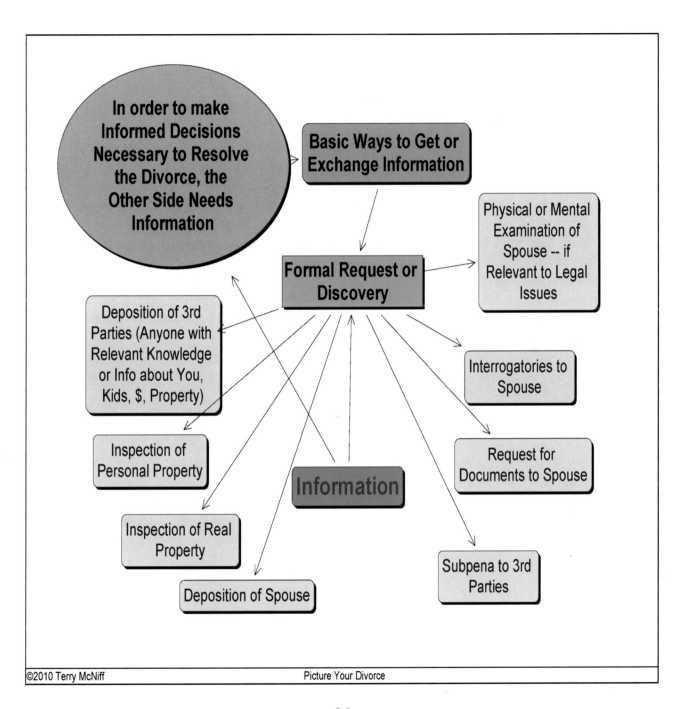

Picture Your Divorce

J. Judges Face Many Limitations You Must Understand Before You Go to Court.

Judges generally do their best to provide justice. But they face limitations. Many litigants – parties in divorce– think before they go to court that once they get to court, the judge has to be on their side. Many litigants think the judge has to be against their spouse. After all, in the minds of most litigants, their spouse is obviously bad, lying, mistaken, or crazy. And many litigants believe everyone should be able to see that fact.

These litigants are often mistaken. No judge tries to take sides. And almost no judge tries to attack 1 side or 1 party. Every judge does her best to appear – and to be – impartial and fair. That basic fact usually means the results in court will end up somewhere in between the two possible extremes. Count on it. And, because of various Constitutional rights, evidence rules, and protections for each party, Courts are limited in what they can and can't hear and do. For instance, they can't transform a bad person into a good person. They can't transform a bad parent into a good parent. They can't make a parent care or always do right by or for the children.

One other thing you can count on with most courts and most judges these days is that they're now very much concerned with administration. As in how many cases they have on their docket or list, how many they disposed of last month or week, and what they need to do to dispose of more cases more quickly. In these times of budgets getting ever tighter, judges and their staff are pinched ever tighter to do more with less more quickly. In that environment, justice suffers. Judges often need to decide quickly with limited or insufficient information.

You can figure out roughly how much time each day a judge has to give to your divorce – not including emergencies. Divide the number of cases assigned for any day by the (available on the clock) court time to reach an average time available. Since 1 or 2 or more cases are calendared for extra time most days, and emergencies are generally not calendared, but do take time, the average will be misleadingly high. But in almost all instances, the average time available per case will be much shorter than you want the judge to spend on your divorce.

Judges rely heavily upon their court staff, especially their court clerks, to administer justice. The court clerks are the backbone of the court, and it is best for you to treat all court clerks and court personnel with respect and consideration for their difficult duties and responsibilities. The court clerks and court personnel deal with angry litigants and abusive lawyers daily, and they know how to get good results in court, so it is generally best to be kind and considerate, and follow their instructions and the court rules at all times.

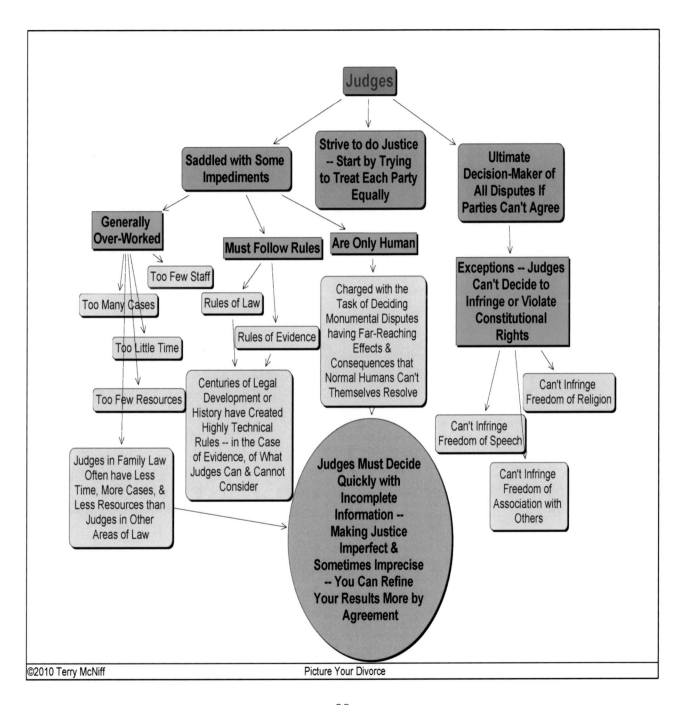

Picture Your Divorce

K.   Kinship.

The main purpose of the picture following is to reinforce the points I've made concerning children. What anyone – and everyone – can see from the picture following is that many people will have an impact on and access to their children. This picture omits many other people who may be involved in the children's lives – teachers, coaches, counselors, therapists, doctors, etc. Even without including these other people who may spend substantial amounts of time with your children, the children seem under attack from all sides by huge numbers – making them hurt.

In a divorce, children are much more heavily impacted negatively than their parents. In almost all cases, the children didn't want the divorce. In most, they feel responsible for it. The children often think the divorce is their fault – or they could have done something to prevent it.

Knowing or learning those facts – that their children feel responsible one way or another – usually stops most parents in their tracks. But many parents in a divorce don't know or believe those facts. Obviously, those 2 facts should be known by – and told to – all parents. So they can help their children.

Another problem is that many parents going through a divorce ignore their children, and their children's needs, at least to some extent. Many parents in a divorce don't know or believe those facts. They don't see it. Or they can't see it. But, it's true, in my experience. And, that's in the best cases – where the parents don't fight actively over the children.

Children need more good attention in a divorce – rather than less attention. And more love and support and nurturing – and hugs and reassurance. Children are usually far more stressed than the adults – but often try to hide their own stress, to protect their parents. Think about that one – children protectively try to hide their own distress when they see their parents distressed.

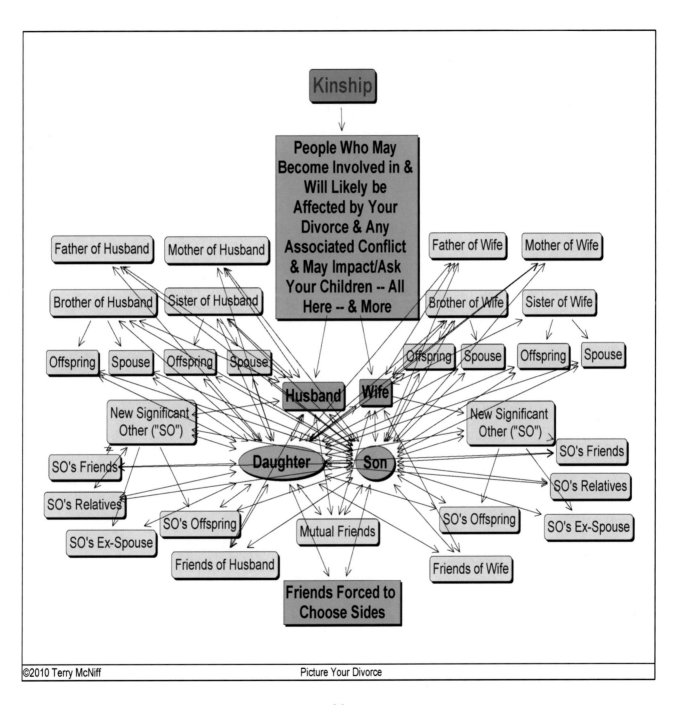

Kinship

People Who May Become Involved in & Will Likely be Affected by Your Divorce & Any Associated Conflict & May Impact/Ask Your Children -- All Here -- & More

Father of Husband

Mother of Husband

Father of Wife

Mother of Wife

Brother of Husband

Sister of Husband

Brother of Wife

Sister of Wife

Offspring

Spouse

Offspring

Spouse

Offspring

Spouse

Offspring

Spouse

Husband

Wife

New Significant Other ("SO")

New Significant Other ("SO")

Daughter

Son

SO's Friends

SO's Friends

SO's Relatives

SO's Relatives

SO's Offspring

Mutual Friends

SO's Offspring

SO's Ex-Spouse

SO's Ex-Spouse

Friends of Husband

Friends of Wife

Friends Forced to Choose Sides

Picture Your Divorce

L.   Legal Issues Overview (Review each section, Custody, Support, Property, for details).

1.   Substantive Legal Issues – Issues Concerning Substance.

In most divorces, there are 3 to 4 main substantive issues, or issues of substance:

- **Child Custody, including decisions, health, education, welfare, time-sharing**
- **Support, including Child Support, Alimony, Maintenance, or Spousal Support**
- **Property, including assets, debts, who gets what, reimbursements, & credits**
- **Fees, including who pays what to whom for the fees of attorneys, experts, etc.**

Child Custody is usually pretty simple. People spend a lot of time, energy, and money fighting about their children (& dogs & cats). But, at the end of the day, except in cases of abuse and/or violence, the court will allow both parents frequent and continuing contact with their children. **Looking at custody from the children's viewpoint, most courts do not want to deprive children of frequent and continuing contact with both of their parents. Unless there's good reason.**

Support is simply the re-allocation of income of the parties. Child support, spousal support, alimony, or maintenance will be ordered in accordance with the communist principle:

From each, according to his or her ability
To each, according to his or her needs

Though most payors (people ordered to pay support) may object, courts in most states can order alimony. Most courts can order 1 side to pay fees to the other too, based on principles used for support.

Property issues generally invoke the equitable principle that parties to a marriage should share marital property – property acquired in the marriage. And marital debts. Complications and exceptions exist, which vary from state to state, but most judges will usually order marital property shared.

91

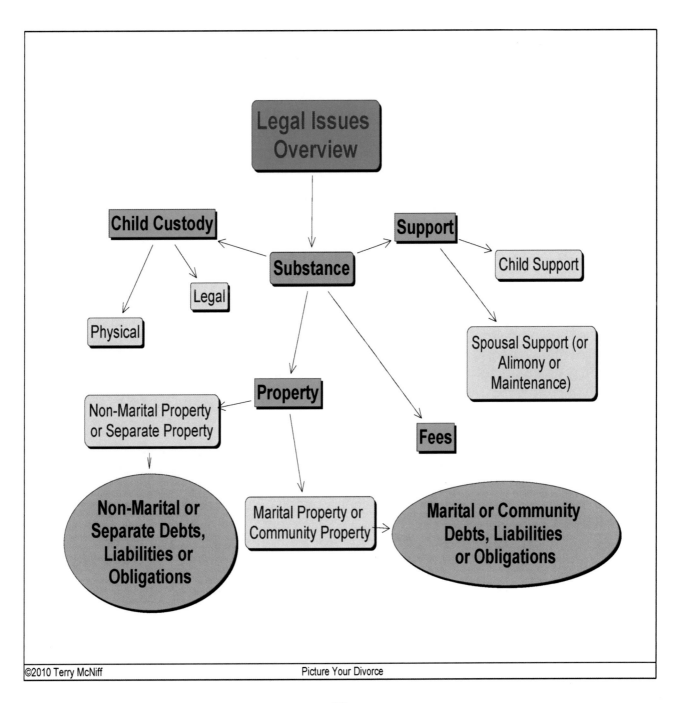

Picture Your Divorce

2. Procedural Legal Issues – or Issues Concerning Procedures.

Procedural Legal Issues are the issues concerning how and when a case is resolved. If your divorce is being resolved by a process other than litigation, then the procedure for your process is a function of the alternative dispute resolution process you selected. (Please see section D. Dispute Resolution Methods, above, for more information about dispute resolution.)

If your divorce is being resolved by way of traditional litigation, then the main procedural issues are identified in the picture following. There are 2 main issues concerning procedure.

The first main procedural issue is the particular stage of your divorce. The stage of your divorce can generally be **beginning, middle, end, or after your divorce**. The procedures available during any particular stage are sometimes governed by the particular stage, but for the most part, after the beginning, and before the end, the procedures available during that interim period are similar. Most of the formal procedures in traditional litigation involve many specific details about the time, place and manner of using the procedures, and about giving advance notice to others, especially the other party or parties, about your use of the procedures.

The second main procedural issue concerns the major types of procedures that are available to the parties after the beginning and before the end of their divorce, and those available procedures are primarily of 1 of the following 3 types:
- **Discovery**, usually a self-executing process for discovering material information, except it's not so self-executing when people decide to fight about the discovery of material information
- **Applications or Motions or Petitions to the Court for relief** involving any substance or any procedure, and the pleadings (writings containing legal arguments) that concern them
- **Hearings or Trials or Agreements, resulting in Orders, Judgments, and Decrees**

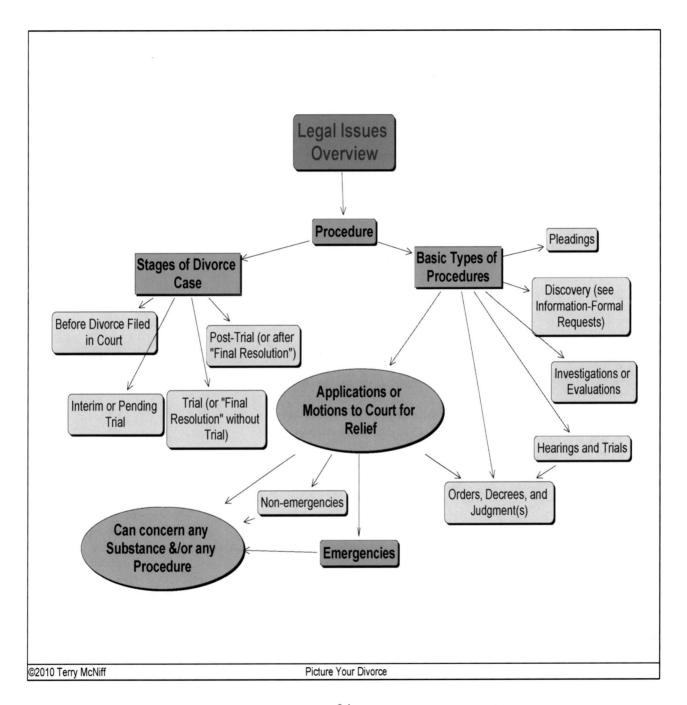

Picture Your Divorce

94

M. Myths of Divorce You Should Understand – Don't Believe Everything You Hear.

The following picture highlights just a few of the more common myths about divorce. If you want to know more myths, just look at popular media or ask any normal person in your circles of friends, acquaintances, or colleagues. Most likely, anything normal people (who are not divorce lawyers) tell you (or what you see in media) is more likely to be at least partly myth than it is to be completely factual.

Let me repeat that because most people find it hard to believe or see. Most likely, anything normal people (who are not expert divorce lawyers) tell you is more likely to be more myth than fact.

If I had a nickel for every time someone told me in advance that their divorce just had to go or end up a certain way – usually, their way – and no other way, because their sister, brother, friend, mom, dad, etc., told them so, I'd be very rich indeed.

Most lay people or normal people are ignorant about the divorce process on at least some level. What that means – what being ignorant means – is one lacks knowledge of the important information. Or the most critical information. And what people don't know can – and usually does – hurt people they love and those dealing with divorce. One thing you can usually count on in your divorce is that it won't go exactly the way your buddy Jim's or Sally's divorce went. Or just like Aunt Edna's. Or Uncle Charlie's. The sooner you realize that simple fact of divorce life, the better it is for you.

Also, realize that whatever anyone other than an actual experienced expert with duties to you tells you about divorce may not be true or may not apply in your case. Unless your actual certified specialist expert tells you the same thing. Most non-experts claiming to know key things about divorce actually only know enough to be dangerous. So, be careful who you listen to and who you trust.

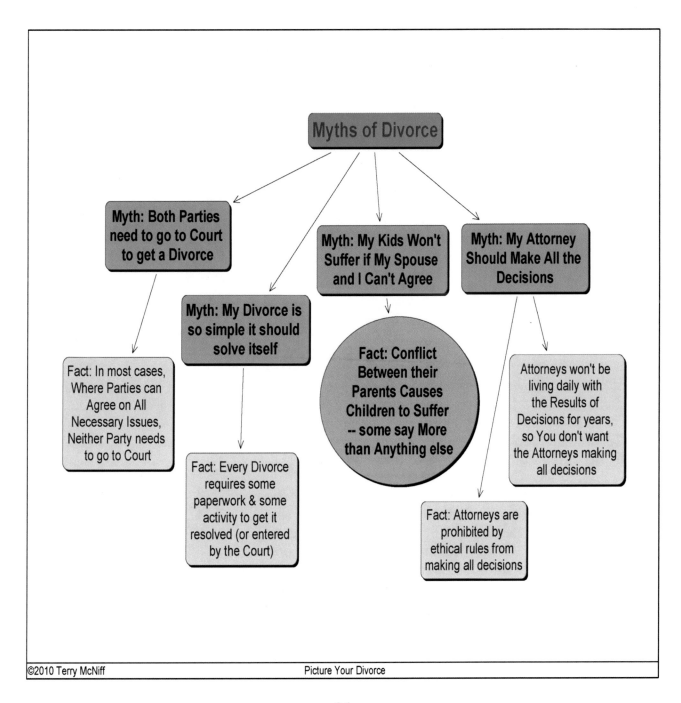

Picture Your Divorce

N.   No-Fault Divorce Makes Divorce Generally Available to Either Party.

In almost all states these days, either party is essentially entitled to divorce their spouse – without actually claiming or proving the other spouse is at fault. That right to divorce is often referred to as No-Fault Divorce. Most states have enacted No-Fault Divorce laws providing neither party is required to prove the reason for the divorce is the fault of the other spouse.

What that means practically is that most courts will not require (though many may allow) inquiry into the bad faith or bad conduct of the other spouse, in the divorce context, unless:
- The conduct at issue includes abuse or violence, assault, battery, etc.;
- The conduct is material to the health, safety, or welfare of the children;
- The conduct interferes with or harms the other spouse in other demonstrated ways, for example, financially, as in breaches of fiduciary duty or fraud costing the other party

The fact that divorce is no-fault in most states can upset some people – sometimes hugely. Some people find it hard to believe – and even harder to accept – that their spouse's horrible (to them) misconduct may not be relevant to getting a divorce. If you're in one of those states that allows divorce for mere "irreconcilable differences", and does not, in ruling on a divorce, punish the other spouse for misconduct of the type you believe your spouse committed, one of the best things you can do to help yourself deal with that fact, is to accept it. Failure to accept it will cause you great unhappiness and more stress you don't need. So, figure out how it works where you live, and accept it. Or suffer more.

Do not confuse No-Fault Divorce – and acceptance of it – with the issue of whether a spouse can recover against the other spouse for various bad acts. For instance, most states allow spouses to sue each other for tort claims arising from the spouse's bad acts. Torts include assault, battery, intentional infliction of emotional distress, invasion of privacy, fraud, negligence and other various claims. Check your state's law for the details. Fault is also relevant to alimony or property division in many states.

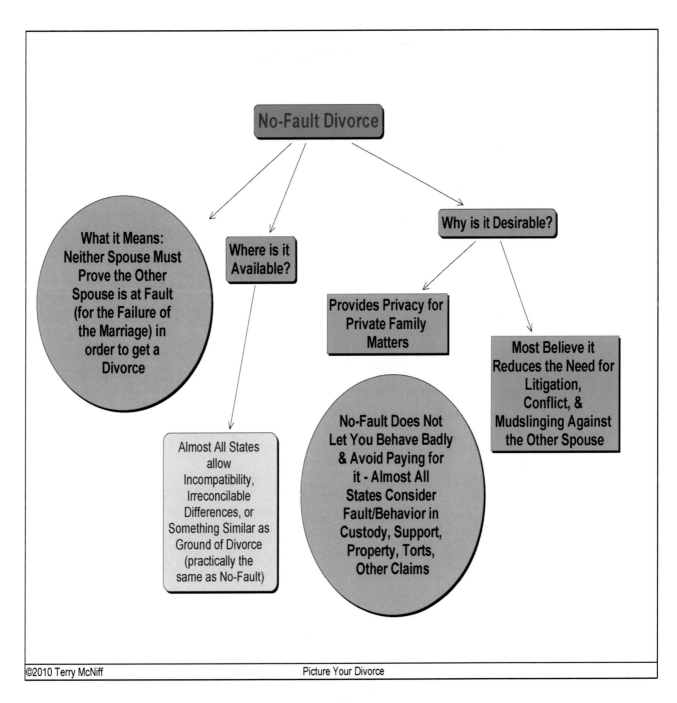

No-Fault Divorce

What it Means: Neither Spouse Must Prove the Other Spouse is at Fault (for the Failure of the Marriage) in order to get a Divorce

Where is it Available?

Why is it Desirable?

Provides Privacy for Private Family Matters

Most Believe it Reduces the Need for Litigation, Conflict, & Mudslinging Against the Other Spouse

Almost All States allow Incompatibility, Irreconcilable Differences, or Something Similar as Ground of Divorce (practically the same as No-Fault)

No-Fault Does Not Let You Behave Badly & Avoid Paying for it - Almost All States Consider Fault/Behavior in Custody, Support, Property, Torts, Other Claims

Picture Your Divorce

O. Orders, Judgments & Decrees Require Special Analysis and Attention.

Many people in a divorce find it hard to accept court orders or judgments or decrees. If you're one of those people, change your state of mind. Learn to accept court orders and judgments. Courts will punish people in a divorce who fail to obey their orders or judgments.

When a court makes an order or judgment or decree, that court is taking a position – that the party or parties ordered to do something should and must do that something. Or, the court is taking the position that the party or parties ordered not to do something should or must not do that something. When you take the opposite position, you don't generally endear yourself to the judge who made the order. In other words, it's highly likely that you are not making the judge happy when you disobey one of her orders. In fact, you'd be making the judge very unhappy.

Some judges don't forget it when you disobey their orders. Some judges, believe it or not, hold it against you. That's bad. You also need to realize that the judge might have many opportunities to use that bad conduct against you. Courts generally have the power to make orders during and after a divorce – for many years when the case has children, ongoing support, alimony, or undivided property. So, be careful about orders and judgments. Don't hurt yourself.

If you are requesting a court order or judgment – or resisting or opposing such a request – focus on what you want the court to order or not order. Many people encounter severe problems when they fail to be clear and complete in the orders or judgments they request or argue about.

Some orders occur automatically. For instance, when you file for a divorce in most states, the court papers include some automatic restraining orders. Although the judge in your particular case didn't personally rule on those orders and didn't specifically enter those orders specifically against you, most judges will take those orders seriously. So, don't disobey even the automatic orders.

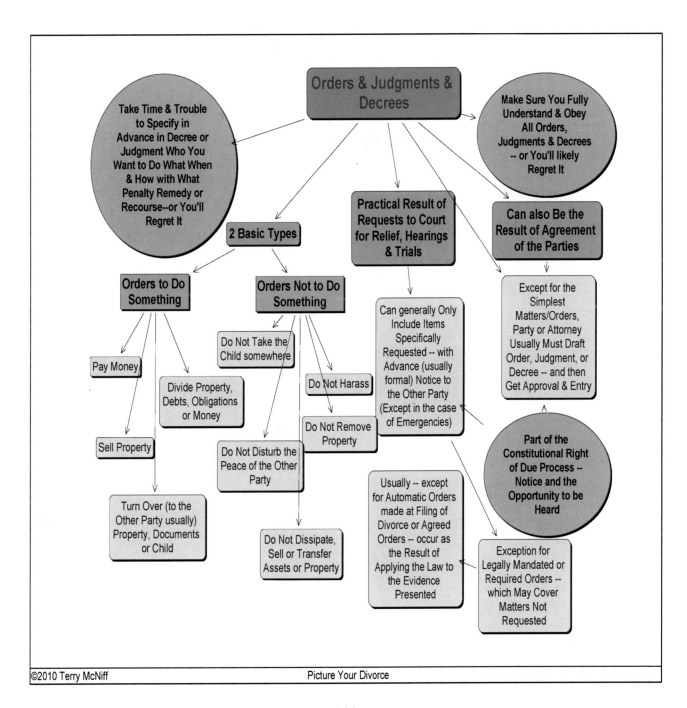

Orders & Judgments & Decrees

Take Time & Trouble to Specify in Advance in Decree or Judgment Who You Want to Do What When & How with What Penalty Remedy or Recourse--or You'll Regret It

Make Sure You Fully Understand & Obey All Orders, Judgments & Decrees -- or You'll likely Regret It

2 Basic Types

Practical Result of Requests to Court for Relief, Hearings & Trials

Can also Be the Result of Agreement of the Parties

Orders to Do Something

Orders Not to Do Something

Can generally Only Include Items Specifically Requested -- with Advance (usually formal) Notice to the Other Party (Except in the case of Emergencies)

Except for the Simplest Matters/Orders, Party or Attorney Usually Must Draft Order, Judgment, or Decree -- and then Get Approval & Entry

Pay Money

Do Not Take the Child somewhere

Do Not Harass

Divide Property, Debts, Obligations or Money

Do Not Remove Property

Sell Property

Part of the Constitutional Right of Due Process -- Notice and the Opportunity to be Heard

Do Not Disturb the Peace of the Other Party

Usually -- except for Automatic Orders made at Filing of Divorce or Agreed Orders -- occur as the Result of Applying the Law to the Evidence Presented

Turn Over (to the Other Party usually) Property, Documents or Child

Do Not Dissipate, Sell or Transfer Assets or Property

Exception for Legally Mandated or Required Orders -- which May Cover Matters Not Requested

P. Property Division.

1. What Factors Does the Court Consider to Divide Marital Property -- & How Do They Work?

Property division is relatively simple in most states in most cases. In most states in most cases, the court will start from the point of view of relatively equal division, or close to it. In most states, the court will be using rules providing for an equitable distribution of marital property. Marital property is generally property acquired during marriage (usually other than by gift or will giving the property to 1 spouse).

In a minority of states, courts will be using community property rules to divide property acquired during marriage. In those community property states, courts are generally required to divide all community property equally. Various exceptions exist in particular circumstances.

I'm not trying to say courts don't make unequal property division orders everyday. It's just that judges generally start from the point of view – when dividing anything – that equal division is most likely to be fair. When requested, the judge will examine the parties' particular situation and facts, and then apply the rules that allow the court to deviate from an equal distribution.

What that should mean to most people is that you need to analyze and examine whether it is worth it in your particular situation to fight about the division of the property. In some cases, it is certainly worth it. And, in some cases, it can be clear that some exceptions to equal division apply. Also, sometimes rules providing for reimbursements, credits, or offsets apply to the facts, and materially change the result. But in most cases, considering the costs, delay, uncertainties, and risks of fighting about it, it is not worth it to fight about the division of most marital property.

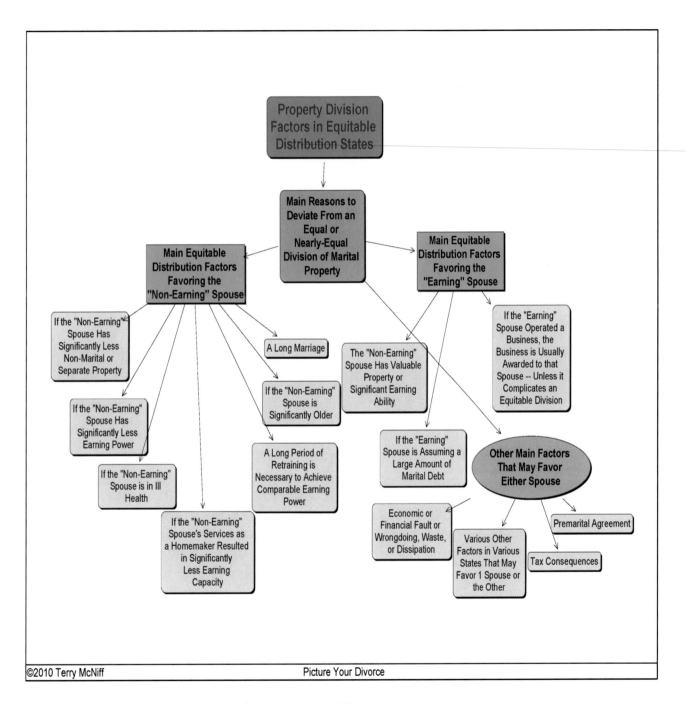

Property Division Factors in Equitable Distribution States

Main Reasons to Deviate From an Equal or Nearly-Equal Division of Marital Property

Main Equitable Distribution Factors Favoring the "Non-Earning" Spouse

Main Equitable Distribution Factors Favoring the "Earning" Spouse

If the "Non-Earning" Spouse Has Significantly Less Non-Marital or Separate Property

If the "Non-Earning" Spouse Has Significantly Less Earning Power

If the "Non-Earning" Spouse is in Ill Health

If the "Non-Earning" Spouse's Services as a Homemaker Resulted in Significantly Less Earning Capacity

A Long Marriage

If the "Non-Earning" Spouse is Significantly Older

A Long Period of Retraining is Necessary to Achieve Comparable Earning Power

The "Non-Earning" Spouse Has Valuable Property or Significant Earning Ability

If the "Earning" Spouse is Assuming a Large Amount of Marital Debt

If the "Earning" Spouse Operated a Business, the Business is Usually Awarded to that Spouse -- Unless it Complicates an Equitable Division

Other Main Factors That May Favor Either Spouse

Economic or Financial Fault or Wrongdoing, Waste, or Dissipation

Various Other Factors in Various States That May Favor 1 Spouse or the Other

Premarital Agreement

Tax Consequences

Picture Your Divorce

2. How Many Ways Can Courts Divide Marital (or Community) Property? 3 Ways.

Courts are usually far more limited than the parties themselves in the particular ways they can order property divided. (Please see the section following this section for 10 ways the parties <u>can</u> generally use to divide property that the court usually <u>can't</u> use to divide property.)

If the court has decided to order an equal division, then the court can divide property (or assets) by 1 of the following methods:

• The court can order an "in kind" division, or an equal division of every major asset or item of property

• The court can order the sale of major assets, with an equal division or distribution to the parties of the net proceeds (net means after subtracting costs of sale, taxes, if any, arising from the sale, and fees and costs incurred for fighting about anything)

• The court can order an asset to 1 party, with a corresponding or equal payment or other asset or assets to the other party as compensation

With any method, the court can generally order one party to pay the other party money to make up the difference. The key thing to keep in mind about any order or agreement for one party to pay the other money is that sometimes people don't make such payments willingly. Or timely. The key thing you need to do – if you are the party expecting to receive money from the other party in return for your interest in marital property (or community property) – is to figure out ahead of time how to force the other party to do so. That may require getting a security interest in the property being awarded to your spouse. Or a bond. Or something else in trust. Don't expect your spouse will always pay willingly.

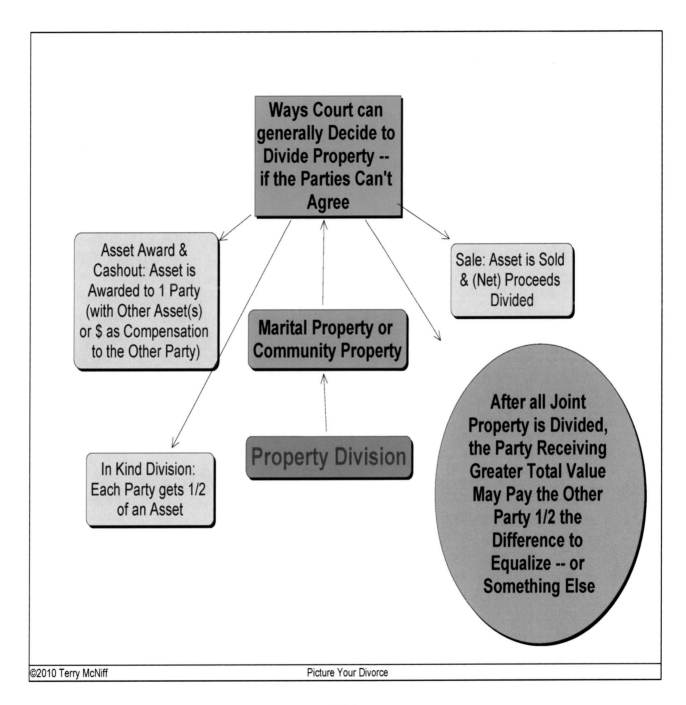

Picture Your Divorce

3. How Many Ways Can Parties Fairly Divide Marital Property? At Least <u>13</u> Ways.

When trying to figure out how to divide their marital property fairly, parties can use any of the dispute resolution methods available for their divorce. (Please see section D. Dispute Resolution Methods.)

Parties can use any of the particular property division methods available to the court to divide their property. But, many people get stuck trying to allocate the various property items between themselves in that fashion. Many times, each spouse wants the same property.

When that happens, and parties reach an impasse, or a dead end, the parties can also use at least **10 specific additional ways to divide the marital property that most people would agree are basically fair**. Those additional 10 ways are identified on the picture following. Considering that the various methods can be combined in various ways, the actual methods available to parties to divide their property fairly are only limited by their imagination and creativity.

Some people seem to feel an irresistible urge to fight over property that can be described as completely unremarkable – and easily replaceable. Don't waste your time or money fighting over pots, pans, non-unique art, furniture, furnishings, fixtures, and all manner of personal property. You're wasting your time or money fighting about those things. Just replace them.

If you reach an impasse, don't just keep arguing about it. Especially don't argue about what's fair or just with most of the personal property. Instead, consider one of the many ways parties can fairly agree to divide property. You can resolve almost all impasses by adopting 1 of the methods in the picture that follows. Eventually, by the time you divide all of the property, you'll see that most of the methods work fine. And, save you from yet another court battle.

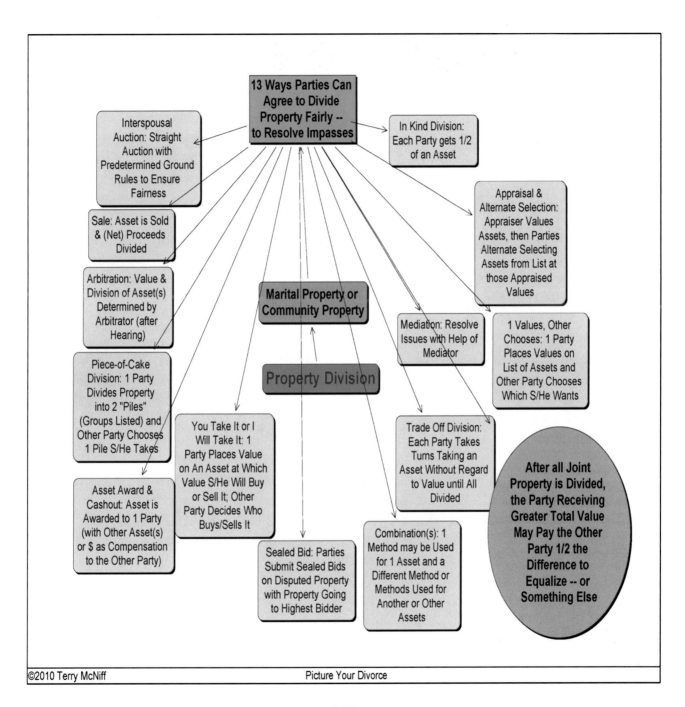

13 Ways Parties Can Agree to Divide Property Fairly -- to Resolve Impasses

Interspousal Auction: Straight Auction with Predetermined Ground Rules to Ensure Fairness

In Kind Division: Each Party gets 1/2 of an Asset

Sale: Asset is Sold & (Net) Proceeds Divided

Appraisal & Alternate Selection: Appraiser Values Assets, then Parties Alternate Selecting Assets from List at those Appraised Values

Arbitration: Value & Division of Asset(s) Determined by Arbitrator (after Hearing)

Marital Property or Community Property

Mediation: Resolve Issues with Help of Mediator

1 Values, Other Chooses: 1 Party Places Values on List of Assets and Other Party Chooses Which S/He Wants

Property Division

Piece-of-Cake Division: 1 Party Divides Property into 2 "Piles" (Groups Listed) and Other Party Chooses 1 Pile S/He Takes

You Take It or I Will Take It: 1 Party Places Value on An Asset at Which Value S/He Will Buy or Sell It; Other Party Decides Who Buys/Sells It

Trade Off Division: Each Party Takes Turns Taking an Asset Without Regard to Value until All Divided

After all Joint Property is Divided, the Party Receiving Greater Total Value May Pay the Other Party 1/2 the Difference to Equalize -- or Something Else

Asset Award & Cashout: Asset is Awarded to 1 Party (with Other Asset(s) or $ as Compensation to the Other Party)

Sealed Bid: Parties Submit Sealed Bids on Disputed Property with Property Going to Highest Bidder

Combination(s): 1 Method may be Used for 1 Asset and a Different Method or Methods Used for Another or Other Assets

Picture Your Divorce

Q. Questions, & Evaluation of the General Resources Available to Find the Answers.

Everyone going through a divorce has questions. Most people going through a divorce or contemplating a divorce have a lot of questions a lot of the time. To get your questions answered, you need to find resources you can trust. Your main resource can be an expert, specialized attorney you consult once (or from time to time) or even hire to represent you.

The first thing to do is to realize you need to be skeptical about resources – & self-styled experts. **Unless the expert you're consulting has been certified by a separate agency that's not selling or promoting anything, you can't know if your potential expert is a real expert.** Never forget that fact.

The best place to start for getting answers is your state court. Your state court is the agency you are required to use if you want to get a divorce. Most state courts are not in the business of selling you products to make a profit. Most state courts want you to succeed in their courts with minimal trouble and expense. And, the state court in your area in your state is the court that will decide all issues you or your spouse choose to fight about.

Your state court is ultimately the court that will decide whether to grant you a divorce. So your state court is the first "go to" resource to get answers to your questions you can trust. For the most part. You don't want to put all your trust in any 1 person or agency. Because even state courts have an agenda. Their main agenda is to administer justice. Or process cases.

You should analyze all other resources you may seek with the understanding most of them are trying to sell you something. You also need to realize the only resource actually accountable to you is an attorney you hire to represent you in your divorce. Only your attorney has ethical duties to you that you can enforce. That doesn't make them perfect, it just makes them more accountable to you.

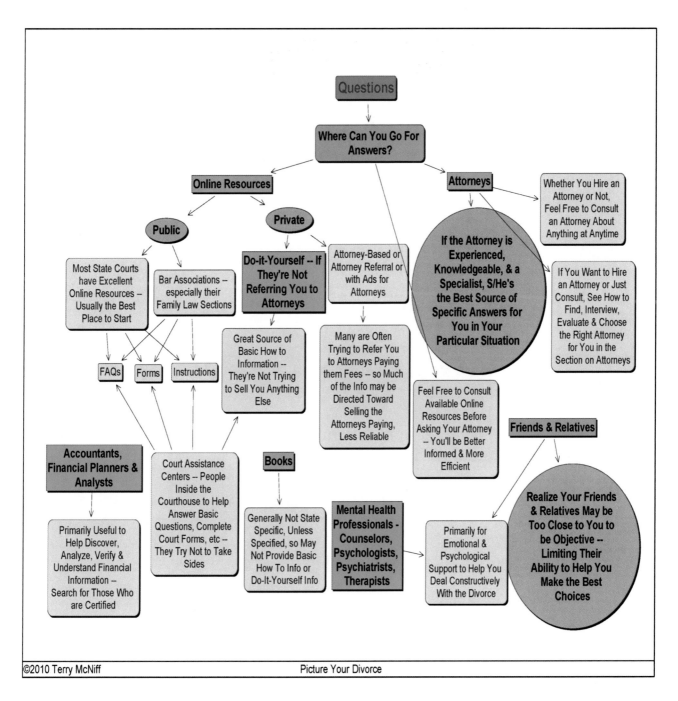

Questions

Where Can You Go For Answers?

Online Resources

Public

Private

Attorneys

Whether You Hire an Attorney or Not, Feel Free to Consult an Attorney About Anything at Anytime

Most State Courts have Excellent Online Resources -- Usually the Best Place to Start

Bar Associations -- especially their Family Law Sections

Do-it-Yourself -- If They're Not Referring You to Attorneys

Attorney-Based or Attorney Referral or with Ads for Attorneys

If the Attorney is Experienced, Knowledgeable, & a Specialist, S/He's the Best Source of Specific Answers for You in Your Particular Situation

If You Want to Hire an Attorney or Just Consult, See How to Find, Interview, Evaluate & Choose the Right Attorney for You in the Section on Attorneys

FAQs Forms Instructions

Great Source of Basic How to Information -- They're Not Trying to Sell You Anything Else

Many are Often Trying to Refer You to Attorneys Paying them Fees -- so Much of the Info may be Directed Toward Selling the Attorneys Paying, Less Reliable

Accountants, Financial Planners & Analysts

Court Assistance Centers -- People Inside the Courthouse to Help Answer Basic Questions, Complete Court Forms, etc -- They Try Not to Take Sides

Books

Feel Free to Consult Available Online Resources Before Asking Your Attorney -- You'll be Better Informed & More Efficient

Friends & Relatives

Primarily Useful to Help Discover, Analyze, Verify & Understand Financial Information -- Search for Those Who are Certified

Generally Not State Specific, Unless Specified, so May Not Provide Basic How To Info or Do-It-Yourself Info

Mental Health Professionals - Counselors, Psychologists, Psychiatrists, Therapists

Primarily for Emotional & Psychological Support to Help You Deal Constructively With the Divorce

Realize Your Friends & Relatives May be Too Close to You to be Objective -- Limiting Their Ability to Help You Make the Best Choices

Picture Your Divorce

108

R.   Reactions Often Determine Where You Go – Watch out for & Avoid Bad Reactions.

Reactions are what you or anyone does in response to stimuli. Stimuli (or in singular form, a stimulus) is anything that happens that provokes, encourages, or causes: (1) something else to happen, or (2) someone to do something. The key stimuli in the divorce context are stimuli a spouse presents or creates. Stimuli from a spouse can be almost anything, including:

- An expression
- A statement
- An action
- A look
- A communication, for example
    - an email
    - a text or tweet
    - a voice mail or phone message
    - a letter
    - a threat
- A motion or application to the court
- A request for information

How you react to the stimuli presented to you often determines what happens next. And where you go from there. Do you want to go where your spouse wants you to go? Or, do you want to go where you want to go? (Remember your goals and the need to avoid detours.)

The choice is yours. So, take a deep breath, reflect on your available choices, and your goals. Once you find a choice that serves your long-term best interests, and goals, then, and only then, should you choose your reaction. Only then can you make a wise choice.

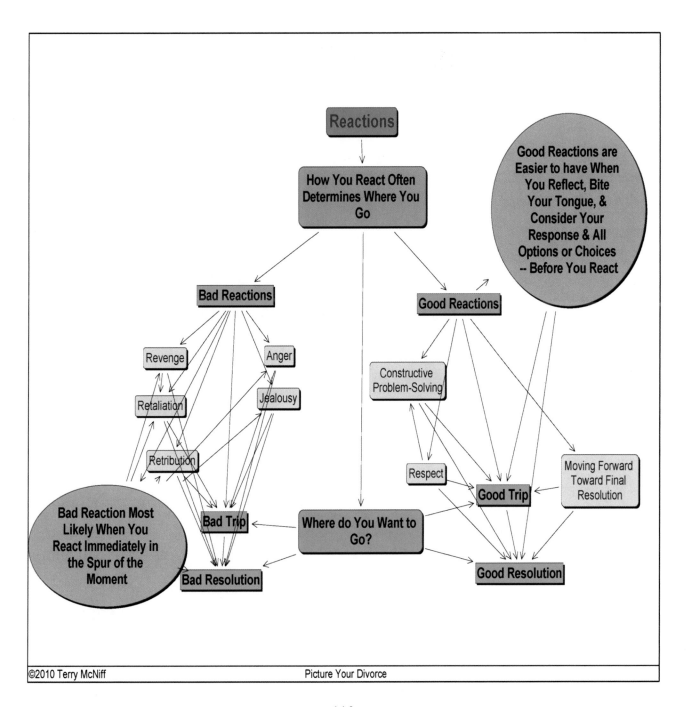

Picture Your Divorce

110

1. Self-Help Reactions or Acts That Are Good.

Self-help comes in 2 forms – like many things – good and bad.

Good kinds of self-help reactions or actions can help you in several ways. First, good kinds of self-help can help you make your divorce easier, faster, and cheaper. Those are very good things. Second, good kinds of self-help can help you realize that you can do good things in times of extreme stress. That's a good thing that can provide comfort to you in stressful situations and events for the rest of your life.

Good self-help also helps your loved ones immensely. When your loved ones see you are getting to work on doing the good things you can do to work through the stress of divorce, they can relax and feel like they don't have to worry quite as much. And, they can devote their energy to positive things, like helping you get through your divorce.

The most positive thing you can do is to gather together the information you need to make sure you know enough to end your divorce fairly and fully. To accomplish this key task, learn enough about the facts and learn enough about the law to determine what's fair and reasonable and necessary.

One thing people generally fail to realize they can do by themselves is to ask directly, informally, for all material information concerning all joint accounts. Instead, many wait and hope their attorney or their spouse gets it for them. You don't need to wait for joint account information. In almost every instance of joint accounts, the holder of the joint account has a duty to provide the information to you – if you ask for it. So, ask for it yourself whenever you can. It's cheaper, and usually faster. If the institution in which the joint account is located fails to provide the information you requested, confirm it in writing. Then, find out your options, because where there's a duty, there's usually a good remedy.

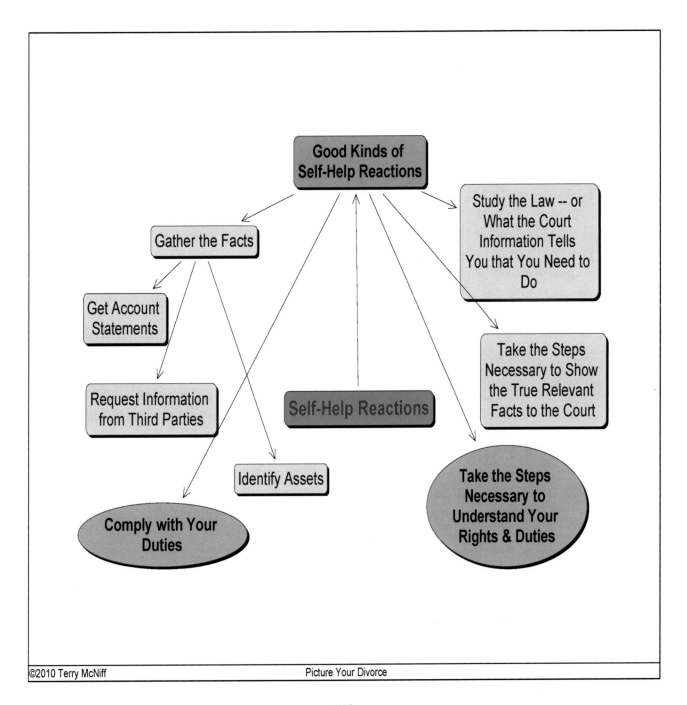

2. Self-Help Reactions or Acts That Are Bad.

You can choose to engage in the bad form of self-help. But, that normally leads to bad things, including a bad trip through your divorce, and a bad resolution of your divorce.

Many people choose to engage in the bad forms of self-help when they become frustrated. Frustration is a common reaction to the divorce process. But, if you let frustration drive you to do things that harm your own best interests, you'll regret it. And, you probably won't reach your worthwhile goals.

As hard as it may be to do, you need to anticipate bad things that may happen, and analyze your options in response to everything that happens – before you act – including the following:

- Your spouse does something you don't like
- Your spouse says something you don't like
- Your spouse fails to do something you want your spouse to do
- Your spouse's (new) significant other does or says something you don't like
- Your spouse's attorney does something you don't like
- Your spouse's attorney says something you don't like
- Your attorney does something you don't like
- Your attorney says something you don't like
- A judge makes a decision you don't like
- A judge says something you don't like
- A judge fails to do or order something you want

You should anticipate all of these things will happen at least once. How you deal with it each time it happens to you is a choice you make – good or bad. It's up to you.

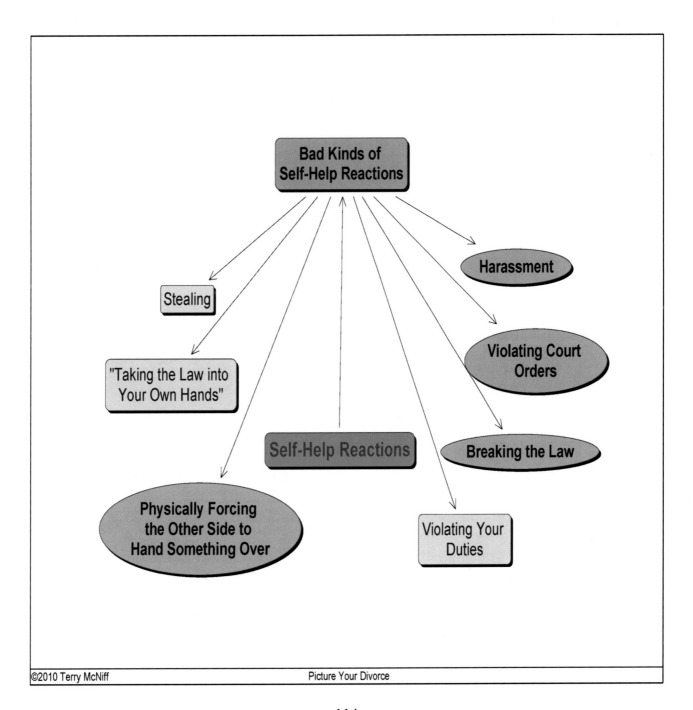

S.　Support.

1.　Child Support.

Child support is a payment made by one spouse (more precisely, by one parent) to the other parent (or sometimes to a third party) for the benefit of a child of both parties. Many parties fight a lot about child support. Most of that fighting is unnecessary and unproductive.

Child support is generally federally mandated or required. Each state is required to have child support guidelines or rules that are mandatory. Mandatory means courts and parents have to follow those rules or guidelines. The guidelines are usually not discretionary or optional.

Some parents use child support, like they use child custody, and their children, as a device to hurt the other parent. They will fight about their income, the other parent's income or earning ability, their timeshare (where that's a factor), and anything they can think of to cause trouble.

Many parents misunderstand or get confused about how child support money may be used by the parent receiving child support. Generally, in most states, with some exceptions, the parent receiving child support is not required to account for how that parent uses child support payments. The main reason for that is that the potential litigation about such disputes could be unlimited, and if allowed, would result in overburdening the courts so they could not function.

There are specific exceptions in specific cases. For instance, sometimes child support payments are ordered or required to be paid to a payee or recipient other than the other parent. For instance, these payees can be medical service providers, such as doctors, dentists, and others. Sometimes, child support is ordered for a specific purpose, for instance, all or part of medical care reimbursements that may be ordered. Or educational expense reimbursements.

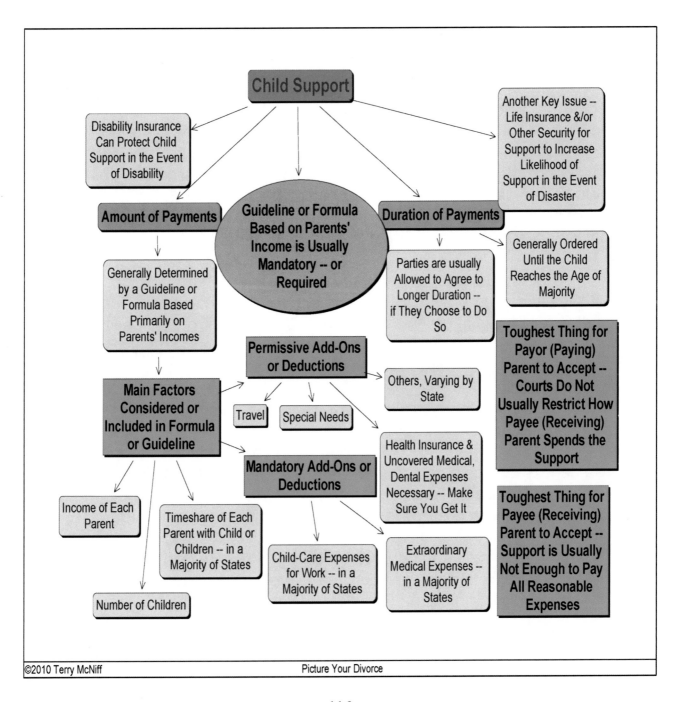

Child Support

Disability Insurance Can Protect Child Support in the Event of Disability

Another Key Issue -- Life Insurance &/or Other Security for Support to Increase Likelihood of Support in the Event of Disaster

Amount of Payments

Guideline or Formula Based on Parents' Income is Usually Mandatory -- or Required

Duration of Payments

Generally Determined by a Guideline or Formula Based Primarily on Parents' Incomes

Parties are usually Allowed to Agree to Longer Duration -- if They Choose to Do So

Generally Ordered Until the Child Reaches the Age of Majority

Permissive Add-Ons or Deductions

Main Factors Considered or Included in Formula or Guideline

Others, Varying by State

Travel

Special Needs

Toughest Thing for Payor (Paying) Parent to Accept -- Courts Do Not Usually Restrict How Payee (Receiving) Parent Spends the Support

Mandatory Add-Ons or Deductions

Health Insurance & Uncovered Medical, Dental Expenses Necessary -- Make Sure You Get It

Income of Each Parent

Timeshare of Each Parent with Child or Children -- in a Majority of States

Child-Care Expenses for Work -- in a Majority of States

Extraordinary Medical Expenses -- in a Majority of States

Toughest Thing for Payee (Receiving) Parent to Accept -- Support is Usually Not Enough to Pay All Reasonable Expenses

Number of Children

©2010 Terry McNiff   Picture Your Divorce

116

2.   Spousal Support, Alimony, or Maintenance.

Spousal support, called alimony or maintenance in some states, is usually discretionary in many ways. Spousal support or alimony is a payment made by one spouse to the other spouse, or for the benefit of the other spouse.

Discretionary means that the court has the power to decide on the particular amount and duration. Within reason. Many states limit their court's discretion to doing only something that is reasonable. Or restrict their courts from doing or ordering anything that is not reasonable.

What that means to the average person is 2 things, practically or realistically speaking. First, it means that it will be harder to predict the precise result where there is greater discretion. That lack of predictability will make it harder to decide what is reasonable. When it is harder to decide what is reasonable, it's also harder to reach agreement.

The second thing it means is that you need to do more homework to see what your particular court or judge usually does in similar situations. An attorney with significant experience and expertise in your particular geographic or court area can usually help give you that knowledge. That knowledge can help you decide what is fair or likely, or at least, help you decide whether what the other side is willing to do is something that is likely for the court to do.

In most states, the court is encouraged or required to consider a long list of various factors to help the court make the key decisions about spousal support – the amount and duration. But, different judges see those different factors in different ways. So, as mentioned above, regardless of the particular factors, the spousal support result is often unpredictable.

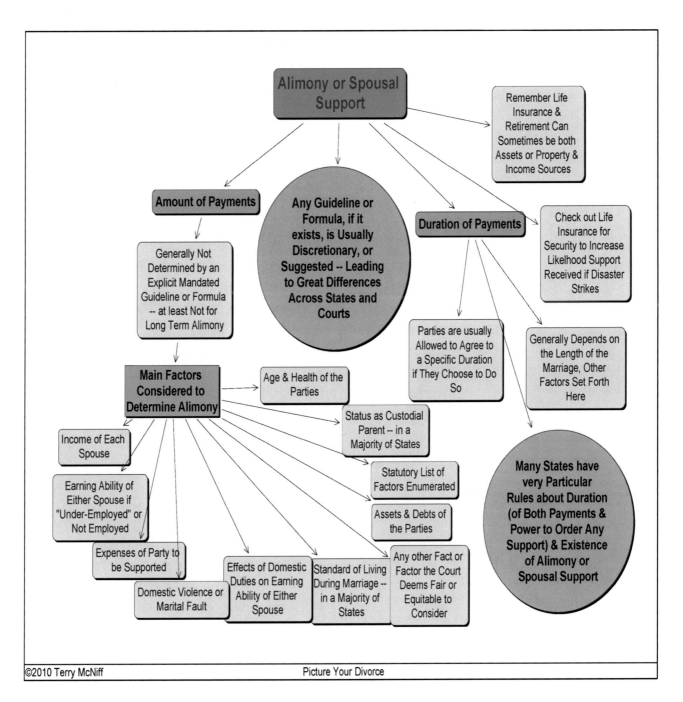

Alimony or Spousal Support

Remember Life Insurance & Retirement Can Sometimes be both Assets or Property & Income Sources

Amount of Payments

Any Guideline or Formula, if it exists, is Usually Discretionary, or Suggested -- Leading to Great Differences Across States and Courts

Duration of Payments

Check out Life Insurance for Security to Increase Likelihood Support Received if Disaster Strikes

Generally Not Determined by an Explicit Mandated Guideline or Formula -- at least Not for Long Term Alimony

Parties are usually Allowed to Agree to a Specific Duration if They Choose to Do So

Generally Depends on the Length of the Marriage, Other Factors Set Forth Here

Main Factors Considered to Determine Alimony

Age & Health of the Parties

Income of Each Spouse

Status as Custodial Parent -- in a Majority of States

Many States have very Particular Rules about Duration (of Both Payments & Power to Order Any Support) & Existence of Alimony or Spousal Support

Earning Ability of Either Spouse if "Under-Employed" or Not Employed

Statutory List of Factors Enumerated

Assets & Debts of the Parties

Expenses of Party to be Supported

Domestic Violence or Marital Fault

Effects of Domestic Duties on Earning Ability of Either Spouse

Standard of Living During Marriage -- in a Majority of States

Any other Fact or Factor the Court Deems Fair or Equitable to Consider

Picture Your Divorce

T.   Temptations & Tensions You Should Resist.

When you feel like you're under attack – which you will feel during your divorce – it's much harder to avoid temptation. Of every kind.

And in a divorce, the sweetest, most enticing temptations are the temptations to inflict pain on your former partner. The sweetest, most irresistible way to inflict pain appears to be to tell off your former spouse in some way. Many people can't resist it. Those who don't regret it.

Whether the temptation comes from anger, jealousy, resentment, hatred, or some other negative emotion, many can't resist telling off their spouse. Most people seem to think divorce is their time to tell off their spouse. Their thinking appears to be that the relationship is over, so it is the time to get even, to get revenge, or to get something off their mind that's bothered them.

One problem with that approach, and mind-set, is that if you have children, as many divorcing spouses do, or if you have continuing duties to your spouse or ex, your relationship with your spouse is not over. Your relationship with your spouse is just entering a different phase. Like any relationship you're involved in, making it a good relationship is a good idea. And, better for you in the long run.

Think about your relationship if it is a relationship that continues. Your relationship with your spouse is not over when you divorce them, if you have children. Your relationship with your spouse is not over when you divorce them, if one of you has to support the other one. Your relationship with your spouse is not over if you co-own property or debt or other liabilities. Your relationship continues. You're joined at the hip, economically. Or otherwise. In any case, it's best if you respect that relationship. If you don't respect that relationship, you'll usually pay the consequences for failing to do so.

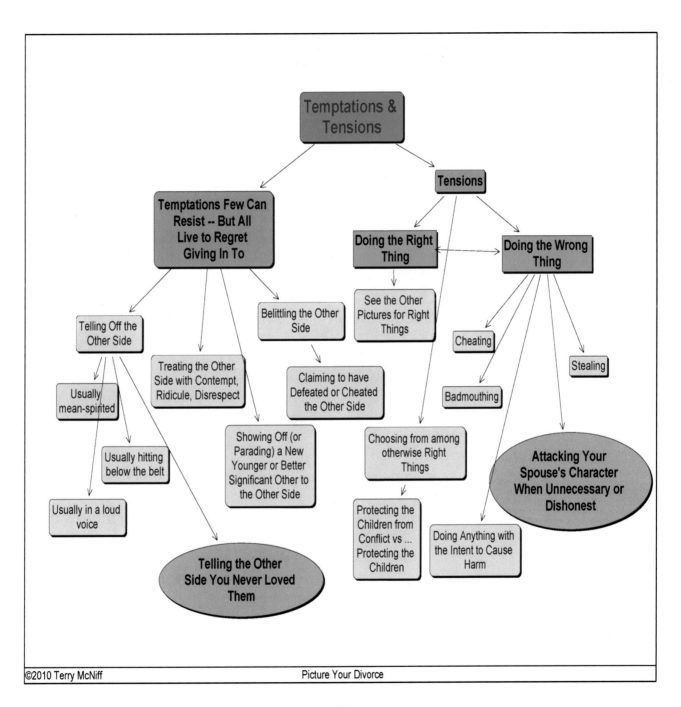

Picture Your Divorce

U.   Undue Influence: What It Is, Why You Should Avoid It, & How to Recognize It.

Undue influence – putting aside the legal technicalities – is basically imposing your will on your spouse through unfair means. Threats. Coercion. Fraud. Or anything similar.

Many people feel all is fair in love and divorce. They feel they can use any tactics they want to get what they want. But, when you have children together, you remain a family unit. You just have different members in different places. And, if you think using undue influence is a good idea when you have children together, go back and gaze at the pictures for children and kinship.

Even when you don't have children together, if you live in one of the (increasingly more frequent) states that punishes you severely for mistreating your spouse physically, mentally, or economically, you'll likely pay the price. That's not a threat or a promise. That's a fact. Somehow, somewhere, sometime, maybe when you least expect it, you'll likely pay the price. The price can often be setting aside a judgment or order or decree or agreement that you thought was cemented in stone long ago. When that happens, or is threatened, it hurts.

I realize the law in some states can become relatively complicated about what is and what is not undue influence. If you're one of those people who has a hard time figuring out what undue influence is, or it's not clear where you live, there's a simple test.

**If you would consider what you're doing to be unfair or sleazy
-- if your spouse did it to you –
that's probably undue influence, or just plain wrong.**

Keep that in mind, and the rest should be pretty easy, relatively speaking.

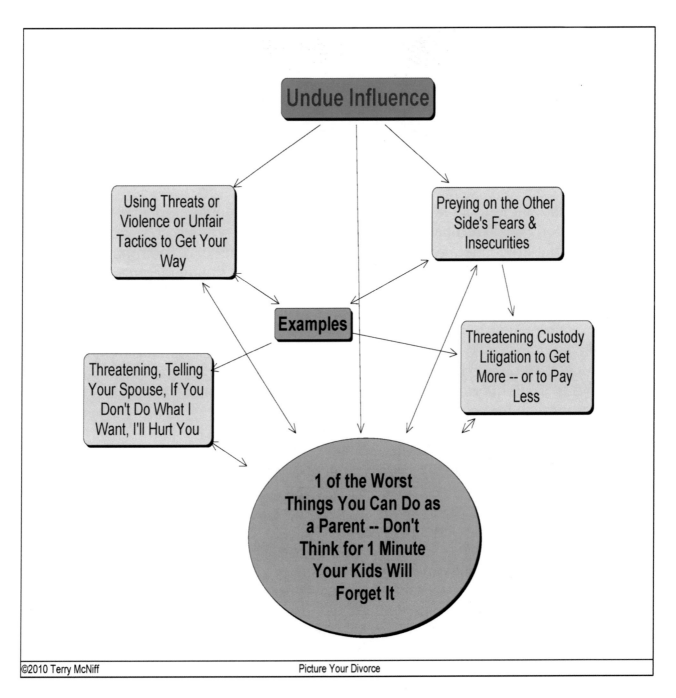

Undue Influence

Using Threats or Violence or Unfair Tactics to Get Your Way

Preying on the Other Side's Fears & Insecurities

Examples

Threatening, Telling Your Spouse, If You Don't Do What I Want, I'll Hurt You

Threatening Custody Litigation to Get More -- or to Pay Less

1 of the Worst Things You Can Do as a Parent -- Don't Think for 1 Minute Your Kids Will Forget It

Picture Your Divorce

V. Visualization Can Help You See the Right Future and Make the Right Decisions.

If you can see it, you can achieve it. If you can see it, you can do it. It's up to you. I know for some people visualization seems like a dream or a gimmick, but unless and until you try it, you'll never know how powerful visualization can be in reaching your goals.

One of the main reasons most people have trouble behaving during their divorce is they don't spend sufficient time or energy visualizing themselves behaving – or visualizing the consequences of failing to behave. Instead, their main focus is their own pain. Or, revenge. And, often, they spend way too much time and energy feeling sorry for themselves.

Our culture tends to reinforce these negative activities, and negative feelings. Behaving badly, and drama, almost always attract more attention than people behaving the way they should behave. And, in a divorce, the people going through it are often starved for attention. They sometimes mistake attention for approval. But, attention and approval are very different.

Self-pity can become an attractive, or irresistible, activity during your divorce. It's just not a productive activity. As almost everyone eventually learns, in order to deal with your divorce constructively, you first have to move on from your self-pity and realize other people have mostly survived their divorce, so you can too. But, you usually have to make it happen yourself.

Once you've moved on from your self-pity, the question becomes what kind of divorce you want to have, and how to go about it. For that, visualization can be very effective. You can visualize yourself being strong, independent, honorable, decent – and you can visualize yourself doing what's necessary to reach a fair resolution. Then you can usually make it happen, regardless of your personal circumstances, if you work at it. It can be done. Many have done it. You can do it too.

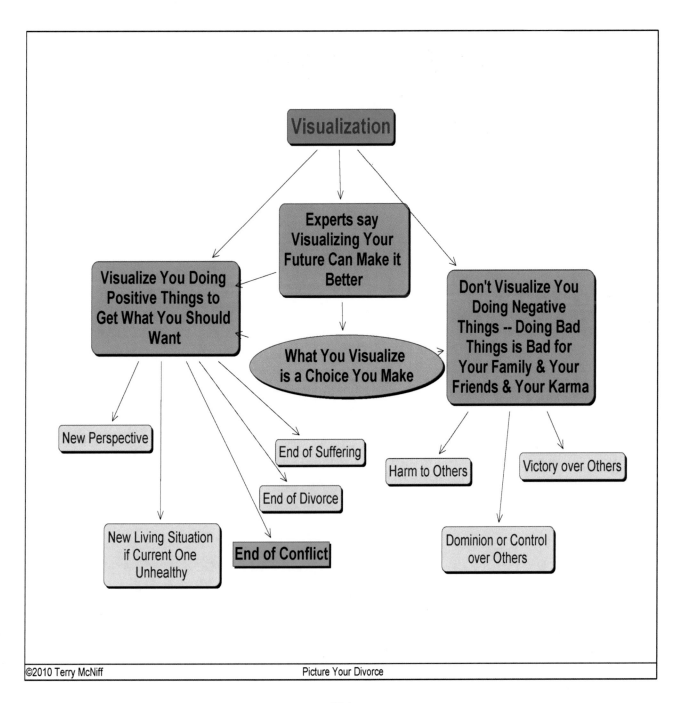

Picture Your Divorce

124

W. Wants & Wishes Often Don't Matter, Unless You Give Something to Get Something.

Wants and wishes are one of my favorite divorce subjects.

Wants and wishes are one of my favorite divorce subjects because they remind me of one of the most powerful moments I've ever experienced in a courtroom.

Many years ago in one of the busiest family law courtrooms in one of the busiest family law courts in the country, a very bright judicial officer made the essence of family law very clear to those before him. The day started out like many before in that courtroom, and divorce courtrooms around the country. Litigants filed into the courtroom, slowly, reluctantly, one by one, until the courtroom was almost filled. Impatient, uncomfortable milling about followed.

Eventually, the judicial officer entered the courtroom. After all present rose and bowed in allegiance to the flag, the commissioner called the first case. The first litigant approached the table in front of the judicial officer, and almost immediately, began whining and complaining about the other side. Commissioner Keith Clemens scanned the audience of those assembled, stopped the whining litigant, and said, for the benefit of all appearing before him in court:

"You need to understand what's going to happen here. Please keep in mind the words of one of the greatest philosophers of the 20th century..." The Commissioner then went on to quote the refrain from the famous Rolling Stones song Mick Jagger and Keith Richards wrote about wants and needs. Like the song, the Commissioner's message was poignant.

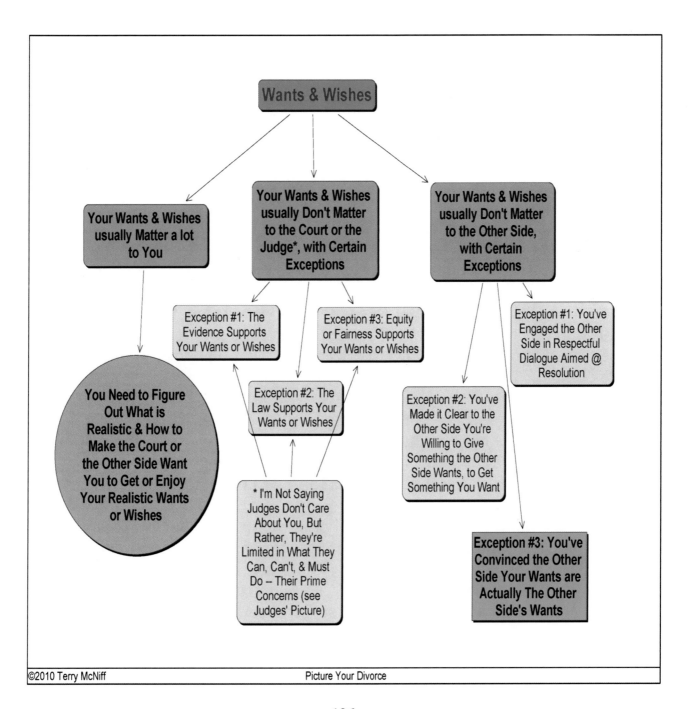

Picture Your Divorce

X.   X Factors Can Be Pivotal in Your Divorce, So You Should Identify Them if You Can.

X factors have various meanings to different people, depending upon who is doing the defining or interpreting. I am using X factors here to reflect those pivotal issues, ideas, or incidents that can turn a divorce definitively toward resolution – or disaster.

For some people, the X factor is something they must have or get for themselves – or must avoid. For other people, the X factor is something their spouse did – that they find unforgiveable. And, thus, a declaration of war.

For others, the X factor is a sore spot. For some, the X factor is a place they can't go. For others, the X factor is a pivotal moment – when they realize they need to resolve their divorce. Or something else they find dramatic or all-consuming.

Whatever it is in a particular case, and however it manifests itself, the X factor may be or become the key thing in your divorce. And the parties in their divorce usually can't see it in the other side. It usually takes a trained, experienced, objective observer to determine the X factor.

And, no matter who accurately determines the X factor, it usually takes a highly-skilled expert to make appropriate use of the X factor to drive the divorce and the parties quickly to resolution. Once you find the X factor in your divorce, everything might become easier. Or, if you mistake the X factor, or use it inappropriately, you can propel yourself and your spouse to divorce disaster, or divorce war. So choose wisely.

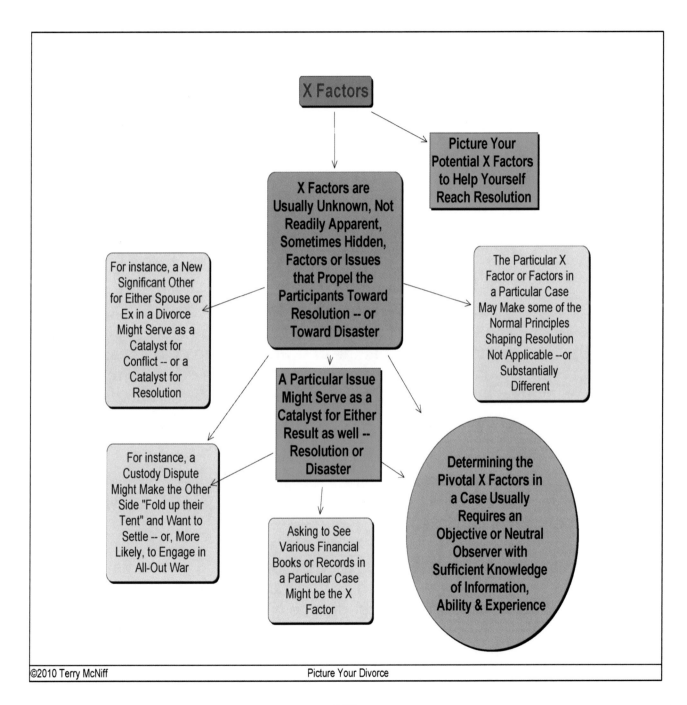

X Factors

Picture Your Potential X Factors to Help Yourself Reach Resolution

X Factors are Usually Unknown, Not Readily Apparent, Sometimes Hidden, Factors or Issues that Propel the Participants Toward Resolution -- or Toward Disaster

For instance, a New Significant Other for Either Spouse or Ex in a Divorce Might Serve as a Catalyst for Conflict -- or a Catalyst for Resolution

The Particular X Factor or Factors in a Particular Case May Make some of the Normal Principles Shaping Resolution Not Applicable --or Substantially Different

A Particular Issue Might Serve as a Catalyst for Either Result as well -- Resolution or Disaster

For instance, a Custody Dispute Might Make the Other Side "Fold up their Tent" and Want to Settle -- or, More Likely, to Engage in All-Out War

Asking to See Various Financial Books or Records in a Particular Case Might be the X Factor

Determining the Pivotal X Factors in a Case Usually Requires an Objective or Neutral Observer with Sufficient Knowledge of Information, Ability & Experience

Picture Your Divorce

128

Y.   You & Your Choices Can Create Your Divorce Consequences.

You are the key factor and actor in your divorce. How & where you go are generally a function of your actions – and your attitude. Whatever you do, you should expect to be met with the same or similar attitude and opposing action by your spouse. Attitudes are contagious.

Remember that bad actions, reactions, and results can begin with the smallest slight. In an emotionally-charged, electric atmosphere like divorce, tiny things often lead to big things. And big things can hurt you & your loved ones for a long time.

So, arm yourself with the best information you can find. Do whatever is necessary for you to get and maintain a healthy attitude. And, then, follow the golden rule. No, not the rule that the one who has the gold rules. The real golden rule. Do unto others as you would have them do unto you. I can tell you from experience that those who follow the real golden rule are the happiest 5, 10, 15, 20, and 25 years later. Those who fought selfishly, or viciously, are the most miserable 5, 10, 15, 20, and 25 years later.

And, it's not even close – for either group. For most people, for most of the time, for most of their life, it's the long-term that matters. Not any momentary, fleeting feeling of victory.

You need to remember that your divorce can be just a moment in your entire life span of many relationships and memories. Or, your divorce can be the defining struggle of your life. Your divorce can break you or define you, but rarely make you happier if you seek to destroy or hurt your spouse. The choice is usually up to you.

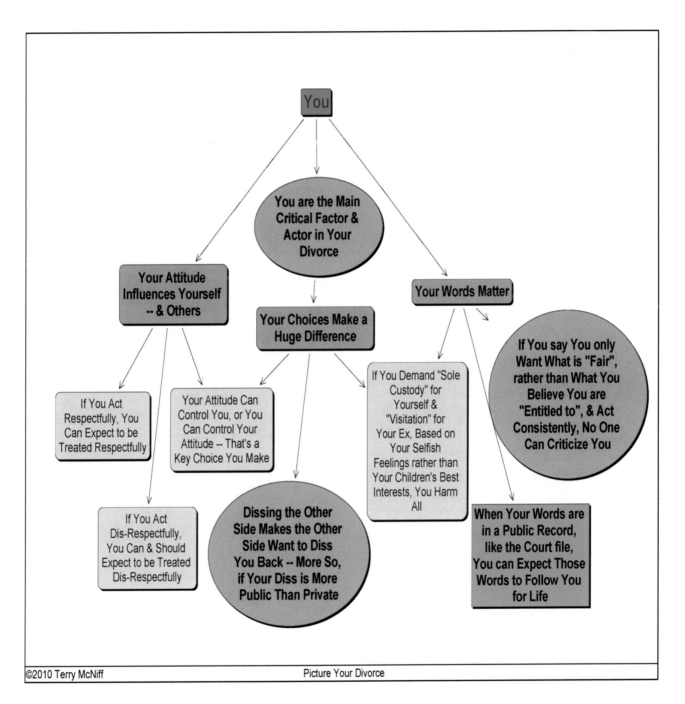

Picture Your Divorce

Z.   Zero-Sum Divorce Games Can Derail or Distract You From Reaching Goals – & The End.

Many people play games in their divorce. That's not surprising. They often play games that don't make any sense. For instance, some people play the game of demanding more than half – of anything – or everything. That is what is sometimes referred to as a zero-sum game.

There are 2 major thoughts about a zero-sum game. The first thought is that a zero-sum game can't be won. Or at least, either participant can't count on winning. The other thought is that a zero-sum game tends to lead to entrenched positions – one side drawing a line in the sand, and the other side daring to cross the line. That's not usually a good thing.

Many people also play another game that in my experience has the same failings and faults as the zero-sum games people play with limited things. That game goes by various names.

The outstanding feature of the game I'm referring to is that each side tries to outdo the other side in putting down or disrespecting their spouse. The first side might start with a snide remark about the other side's parenting skills – or lack thereof. Or the first crack might be about the other's general – or specific – alleged lack of character. Or alleged lack of morals. Or alleged lack of honor. Or something similar.

The other side takes the remarks or positions of one side as a direct attack on their entire being. As a result, the side scorned or disrespected must outdo the other side. And, thus the battle of words begins. It usually ends with both sides thoroughly defeated or ashamed. But only after huge conflict and expense – costing both parties hugely. Don't play those games. Or, most likely, you'll live to regret it. Over and over. Especially, if you have kids. Kids remember.

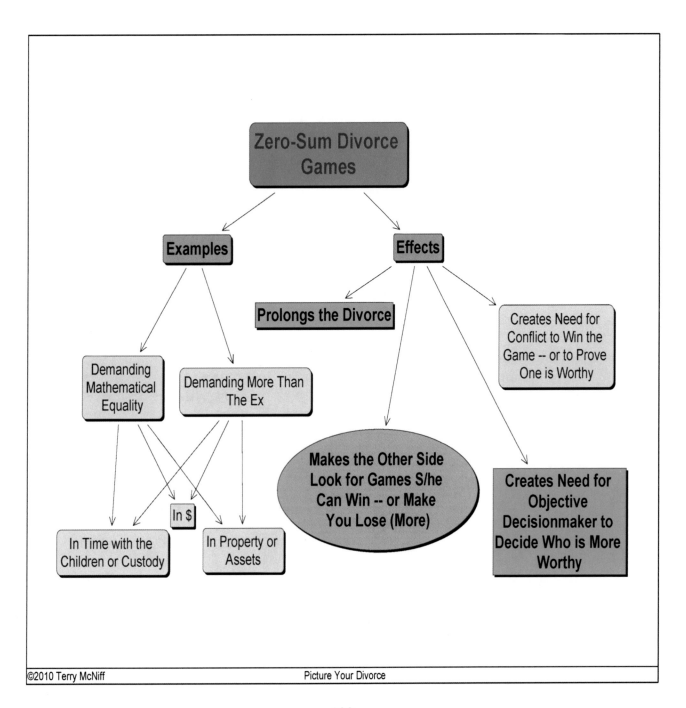

Picture Your Divorce

III.   Acknowledgments

For those of you going through divorce, I feel I need to warn you that nothing in this section of the book may help you in your divorce. There may be nothing here in this section to help you see. I also have to warn you there may be information in this section that might make you feel bad or sad. This section is the part where I thank and acknowledge the many people who have helped me to see all there is to see, to reach my potential, and to work for decades in a demanding field that many people look down on or criticize. I believe this section is necessary because many wonderful people have helped me in my professional life, and I need to acknowledge and thank them. My mom taught me that's the right thing to do; I have to thank those who have given me gifts. However, I can remember many times during divorce when it felt like almost all of one's friends and family had abandoned one in the midst of one's greatest hours of need – or worse, had gone over to the dark side – so I can recognize this part of the book could make you feel resentment, jealousy, anger, and other bad emotions that won't help you. Therefore, please heed my warning and skip this section if you are in the midst of your divorce, and the happiness of others depresses you.

On the other hand, for those of you who decided to read this section, I'm not including this thanks part selfishly. I believe this part may help you see that even after your divorce, you could realize you have many reasons to be grateful. Gratefulness is a wonderful feeling, and I can guarantee you that gratefulness is possible in your future.

This guide arises from the people who helped me picture and write it: clients, family, friends and colleagues. My wife, Prescilla, is first and foremost responsible. She pictured the title. She supported me while I was writing and picturing this guide, and provided valuable thoughts and suggestions and questions. She's the nicest, best person I know, and I am extremely fortunate to have her in my life. Prescilla has been more supportive and loving than any person has a right to expect, or to receive. I have been blessed beyond anyone I know to have her in my life.

I have also been blessed by the efforts and influence of many other special people in my life. Most of those people had nothing to do with this book, but a great deal to do with my professional development. Many of those people have been prominent, successful, popular lawyers. Since this book is a guide for clients in legal divorce disputes, the influence of those lawyers has been monumental. To have had the good fortune to meet and work with one of these lawyers would have been more than enough for anyone.

First and foremost among the lawyers who blessed me with their time and example is Dave Kagon, my original mentor. Dave was loved by many, and respected by all who knew him. Dave was the best lawyer I've ever known. Dave taught me everything I needed to know to be a decent lawyer, almost always by example. Two key things Dave taught me he expressed verbally, one about caring, and one about decisions. About caring for clients, Dave said that if you are a conscientious, dedicated lawyer, your main worry has to be caring too much. As Dave explained it, the lawyer offered to the client mainly objectivity and good judgment. If the lawyer became too close to the client or the client's cause, the lawyer lost objectivity. Without objectivity, the attorney was no longer an asset, but instead had become a liability. About decisions, Dave taught me that decisions are pretty easy to make if you remember there is only one thing that matters, and that is, do the right thing. Dave's wife, Dottie, a great artist, and a wonderful person, always treated me and my family warmly, as part of her own family, and we'll be forever grateful for her many kindnesses.

My second mentor, Paul Gutman, was both the most highly-skilled lawyer I ever met, and also the funniest. Paul had worked the borscht belt circuit (in the Catskills) before becoming a lawyer, and he often demonstrated those marvelous joke-telling skills. Paul was precise in his use of language, and in his knowledge and application of the many technical rules constricting lawyers at trial. Paul was also a warm, wonderful person who went on to become a great judge after our years working together. I can't mention Paul without thinking of his better half, Diana. Diana was the best business-person and office manager I've ever known. Diana made it possible for Paul to concentrate on just the law and representing the clients, because Diana expertly handled everything else. Paul and Diana were both exceptionally generous to me with their time, patience, and consideration.

David and Paul have recently both passed on, leading me to think more deeply about them, and especially about how I can best honor them and their legacies as exceptional divorce lawyers and human beings. David and Paul both saw the law as something of a sacred institution in human development. In their view, the rule of law is what separates us from terrorists, dictators, anarchy, disorder, repeated violent civil wars or internal wars, violent protests, persecutions, and similar bad things. Law is what stops some humans from getting -- & using – their own individual or parochial power to destroy, harm and abuse other humans. Law can – and does – help us be civilized, so we can study, learn, become educated, and research and resolve the most compelling & urgent problems of the day, and the world. Law makes that possible. Where the law is fair and accessible. In some cases, many cases actually, I have seen many involved say the law is not fair. Or not accessible enough. To some extent, sometimes, this is true. But, for the most part, the law strives to be fair and accessible – at least in a great nation.

The shining example David and Paul provided to me and others compelled me to write this book to honor them. I hope my contribution can make the law more fair and more accessible for many people who need the help of the law. I hope this book gives the memory of David and Paul and their long service and devotion to the law the justice they deserve. This book arises from their thoughts and their service, devotion, and great decency and consideration.

Richard Witkin, who was the director of the UCLA student legal services clinic where I first had the opportunity to represent clients, was also instrumental to my development of legal skills. Richard taught me, among other things, that persistence and perseverance can often trump or defeat mere talent and intelligence. And, he also taught me the client comes first.

Arlene Falk Withers taught me trial advocacy at UCLA, and she challenged me to be the best advocate I could be. She never let me take the easy way out, and she inspired me to work hard and learn enough so I could be an effective advocate for clients.

Bob Kahan, an exceptional business lawyer, also served as a mentor, though we did not practice law together. When I was a young lawyer, Bob entrusted to me the resolution of a personal problem for one of his clients. When I managed to find the right solution, using what David taught me, Bob's client prospered. And Bob showered me with praise. Going out of his way to inform the partners at my firm what a great thing he thought I had done, Bob gave me a great gift. Bob was also the best 40-something center fielder in our lawyer's softball league.

Rich Pachulski, a great bankruptcy lawyer, businessman, and strategist, similarly provided early critical, generous mentoring. Rich referred a client to me, also, like Bob did, in the early years before most inexperienced lawyers like I was at the time should expect referrals of that level of client. With Rich's help, we were able to solve the client's problem, despite the extremely strong, destructive emotions of both parties, and despite other serious difficulties. Rich also mentored me at various critical points throughout my career, always with his kind, generous, upbeat manner and enthusiasm.

Mike Michel, an early opponent on a divorce case, also provided inspiration and mentoring. Mike and I respected each other after going head to head in a case that became hotly contested. But for his better half, Karen Rhyne, also an exceptional divorce lawyer, we probably wouldn't have become, and stayed, good friends. Karen, like my wife, is not just a fine lawyer, mother, and multi-tasker, but also, Karen somehow keeps her many friends and family firmly ensconced in her large, friendly circle, planning and executing great adventures, trips and get-togethers. Karen and Mike have both shown us for over 20 years that you can be extremely busy as a lawyer, but still have fun and adventure.

Dan Burke, the best divorce trial lawyer I've seen in San Diego County, also gave very generously of his time and talents, helping to make me a better lawyer and a better person.

Dan and his wife Susan, a great artist and teacher, have generously given many benefits to me and my family, far beyond what any person could hope for.

The list of lawyers above is by no means exhaustive. What I've said about each of them does not begin to capture everything good or wonderful they have done for me. But I want to acknowledge them, nonetheless, because I am extremely grateful. And because of their example, I am compelled to give to others.

Many others have also given wonderfully of themselves. They include other lawyers, like Don Mike Anthony, the most honorable lawyer I know; Sterling Myers, and his wonderful assistant Jo, a great team for their clients; David Wheeler, one of the finest, most refined trial lawyers I've ever seen; and Jan McDonald, a great mediator and friend.

I'd also like to acknowledge and thank Dr. Larry Rosen, the expert on the psychology of technology, especially as it relates to reaching and teaching young adults, author of the groundbreaking educational work *Rewired: Understanding the iGeneration and the Way They Learn*, and other works. Similarly, I'd like to acknowledge and thank Dr. Jaime Romo, author of a powerful work, *Healing the Sexually Abused Heart*, and an experienced educator in his own right, a teacher of teachers. Dr. Rosen and Dr. Romo graciously shared with me separately their individual knowledge and experience in education, writing, and publishing.

I also benefitted greatly from many wonderful professors during my formal education who inspired me to love learning for life, as they showed they did, and enjoyed it immensely, including Chuck Chalberg, Mulford Q. Sibley, John R. Howe, Jr., Paul L. Murphy, and many others.

And, last but certainly not least, I am most grateful to my clients. Each one of them has taught me something important. And each one has survived, persevered, and when they set about to do so, prospered. My ethical and professional duties to those clients bar me from revealing their secrets, or anything else about them. But they know who they are, and what they've done. To each of them, I hope this guide says thanks.

None of the folks I've acknowledged are responsible for anything in this book. None of the folks I've acknowledged (outside my family) have even seen this book, or the pictures in it. I'm solely responsible for all omissions and errors, and the entire contents and ideas.

All of the folks I've acknowledged went above and beyond the call of duty reaching out to me in a meaningful way. For none of them was their own self-interest or profit their main motivation. For that and them, I am forever grateful.

IV. Disclaimers

This section is the part where I explain in clear terms that this book cannot get you divorced. It can only help you make your divorce better and easier. This book also can't save you from getting divorced, if your spouse wants to divorce you. It can only help you see how to deal with your divorce to make it better and easier, showing you what to expect, your main options, and the likely consequences.

This book does not contain legal advice. This book contains practical advice, tools and information to help you see. The author of this book highly recommends you get as much legal advice as possible – as often as possible.

You should not rely on this book to solve any particular legal problem. If you want to solve any legal problem, the author highly recommends you get as much legal advice as possible – as often as possible. Getting good legal advice requires that you first establish a client-attorney relationship with an expert, experienced attorney, and second, that you disclose to that attorney everything that might be relevant to your legal problem(s), including a complete, well-developed, accurate history of your entire relationship with your spouse, and everything else pertinent. That's necessary because many things are related to many other things, especially in the law and in divorce. Then, you need to pay your experienced attorney to take the time and trouble to fully analyze your personal situation and all of the facts, apply to your personal situation all of the applicable law and legal principles existing in your particular jurisdiction, and then create a complete written legal analysis of your problems, the potential solutions, the potential consequences, and your attorney's recommendations for you.

This book may be utterly useless, or at least, potentially less useful, in your specific personal situation. For instance, if your ex is hell-bent on your destruction, this book might not be as useful to you as it is to a person whose spouse is not hell bent on their destruction.

Similarly, if you are hell-bent on your own destruction, this book might be less useful to you.

Also, if you are hell-bent on your ex's destruction, this book would tend to interfere with your greatest hopes and dreams.

This book is intended to guide individuals faced with the daunting prospect of divorce to see how to make good decisions. This book is not intended to supersede or replace the many excellent guides to divorce law, divorce practice, divorce procedure, and divorce psychology.

Many state courts provide excellent step-by-step instructions for the mechanical steps necessary to obtain a divorce. This book does not provide the particular mechanical steps, and does not contain the specific paperwork needed to get a divorce in any jurisdiction or state. Rather, this book is a practical guide to see and learn how to make good decisions – before, during, and after divorce.

The author believes the many excellent guides existing as of this initial writing and picturing that concern the subject of divorce are less accessible and less useful to individuals undergoing divorce, partly because most such guides are very dense, very long, and heavily rely on war stories and anecdotes of other people's divorces. Each person going through a divorce has a divorce experience that is unique to that person. So what each person undergoing divorce needs is both a guide and a manual she or he can use to see and create a better future – not just a bunch of words telling them what to do.

This guide is intended to be a starting point for learning about the key issues and decisions in divorce – along with the likely or potential consequences of various decisions. This guide does not include every factor or nuance of all laws in all states. Rather, this guide contains a reference to most of the general legal principles applicable in most states to most divorces. In many states, different words are used for some of the ideas and subjects in this book. For instance, child custody is not called child custody in every state. Sometimes, a custody order is referred to as a possession order or timeshare order, for example.

Not everything in this guide applies to every person, every situation, every divorce, or every state. For instance, if you don't have children – or you object to this guide's focus on children – please consider that other people in your life will generally also be affected by your divorce. And, other people will be affected by your decisions in your divorce.

Also, please understand this guide focuses on children because too many parents fail to focus on their children, in the author's experience. Too many parents allow their children to become victims of an unnecessarily bitter divorce. But, we can all agree the children who are victimized by their parents in bitter divorces are certainly innocent victims. For that reason, this guide stands up for children. This guide focuses on and supports the children of divorce, over and over. We can all agree, I'm sure, that we all want to give the parents of the children of divorce every opportunity to see they don't have to make their divorce bitter, and to understand they shouldn't make their divorce bitter, for the sake of their children.

If you or anyone you know or heard of has heard of or read a disclaimer in any context throughout their lives that is broader or more inclusive than the disclaimers here, those disclaimers are hereby incorporated by this reference as though fully set forth hereat. If not, or if so, all disclaimers ever made throughout human history are included and incorporated by this reference as though fully set forth hereat or herein.

If you have a problem or criticism of this book, please realize that your problem or criticism might be misguided or mistaken. Or, you might be failing to take into account the goals of this book.

The main goal of this book is to help individuals see their way to make better decisions while they go through their own unique divorce experience. In order to help those individuals, this guide contains different pictures in different contexts to appeal to different people – with one major message.

The main message is that each person can make good decisions in their own divorce – better decisions than the many bad decisions I see almost everyday – if they get a little education and knowledge, try hard enough to be smart about helping themselves, and view things from the proper angle or perspective. This book, looking at divorce issues and decisions from many different angles or perspectives over a range of many different subjects with different views, should reach most people with that message.

If we are being realistic, we can't expect every picture, or every part of every picture, or even key parts of every picture to reach out to and touch everyone. People see differently. People see different things in the same pictures. The goal is to reach as many people as possible to help save each of them from unnecessary heartache, pain, expense, and trouble in their divorce.

If we are being realistic, we have to acknowledge that almost no one wants to "picture" their "Divorce" because it's painful – but it's necessary for everyone who wants to do what they can to avoid the biggest, longest-lasting mistakes. If you don't picture what's coming, you're often likely to be caught by surprise, and to become more disappointed and upset. If you don't picture what's coming, you're likely to make big mistakes, like normal people everyday, & like famous people who often make the news for their horrible decisions in the midst of divorce. Do you think a normal person would set off to destroy their spouse or ex if they knew – or could first see before they did it – they were hurting their children more than their spouse or ex? I want to do what I can to help them see first, so they can see how to help themselves.

If you feel the pictures here are not artful or not pretty enough, and therefore are or might be less effective than they could be, I think you might be missing major points. Pictures reflecting ideas don't have to be the prettiest to be effective. Pictures reflecting ideas don't have to be perfect to be effective, either. The pictures and their ideas just need to connect with and touch someone going through their divorce to be effective and useful and thought-provoking. If some of the people going through a divorce give a little more thought to some of their decisions in their divorce as a result of this book, or the pictures in this book, then the book is successful, because the book helped them see.

If you suspect – or even if you feel certain in your mind – that the pictures or ideas expressed here will not help or reach anyone undergoing divorce, then perhaps your view is not realistic, because only a person presently undergoing her or his own divorce can now determine whether the pictures or ideas expressed here help that person. And, they may only see that best or well in hindsight.

If you're having trouble seeing the meaning in these pictures, then maybe you're not going through a divorce, or not contemplating divorce. Or, maybe you've become resistant to the power of pictures because you've become steeped in the tradition of using or seeing only words to convey or receive messages or information or ideas.

If you think some pictures in this book are too simple, or conversely, if you think some pictures in this book are too complex or busy, you should realize the book's pictures are designed and intended to reach large numbers of people with vastly different educational levels, experience, comprehension, intelligence, and viewpoints – at many different stages in their divorce experience. As a result, the book's pictures necessarily should be varied, and should cover or reach out to the wide gamut and array of the potential audience's personal experiences, personal characteristics, and personal viewpoints.

If you think this book can be improved by – or needs – personal examples or anecdotes from actual cases, please understand that the rules of professional responsibility and my own sense of professional responsibility prohibit it. The rules of professional responsibility require me to maintain inviolate and preserve my clients' secrets. My clients expect and deserve complete confidentiality and privacy. As a result, I am not at liberty to present personal stories or reflections of my clients' experiences, even if I were inclined to provide that kind of information. And, I am not so inclined.

If you think this book is too short, you might've missed the message of this book. This book is shorter than some others partly because it contains many pictures, and partly, to inspire the reader to make her or his own personal pictures. This book identifies paths to finding the right answers for each particular reader, primarily through encouraging visualization and picture-making. Picture-making helps decision-making. After all, once you've seen a picture used the way pictures are used in this guide, you can envision for yourself all kinds of pictures – and their contents.

Similarly, if you think this book failed to mention something you consider to be critical in the context of divorce, you might've missed part of the point of this book. This book is a tool to identify the key issues most people struggle with the most in divorce, and to empower the reader to seek and find the answers that matter most to that individual reader, using the power of pictures. Those answers and lessons come best from doing – from working out the solutions with guidance. Not just from seeing. Not just from hearing. Not just from being told what to do. Or not do. Only best from doing.

For you would-be critics, I raise these issues to give you pause. In order to raise the level of dialogue about divorce, I want you too to see why I might have presented certain things in certain ways, or why I might not have presented certain things, or why I might not have used certain ways to present things that you think I should have or could have used. In order to raise the level of dialogue about divorce, I want you too to picture why, what and how.

140

Then, we can all contribute more to help folks who need help to survive and thrive in divorce. That's my goal.

If you have constructive criticisms or suggestions, or if you have benefitted from this book, please feel free to let me know. Like most people, I like to know how I can improve. I would also like to know how I may be able to help more people better. I would especially like to know if you can add to the pictures or thoughts about what else could or should be pictured to help those in divorce. I have devoted most of my professional life to helping people in divorce, because I firmly believe people in divorce need professional guidance they can trust, and many divorcing people suffer without it. Divorce hurts. Please let me know if I have helped you or someone you know deal with and survive divorce difficulties.

I sincerely believe this guide will help more people make their divorce better and easier than the number of people I am able to help only by working one on one representing them as their attorney in their individual divorce. In that sense, I'm sure this guide will be successful. Thanks for reading and seeing.

V.   Bibliography, Useful References & Links

http://PictureYourDivorce.com : the place to find more useful pictures and information to help guide you through your divorce

State Court Websites on National Center for State Courts: the place to link to your particular state's court website to find pertinent forms & information
http://www.ncsc.org/Information-and-Resources/Browse-by-State/State-Court-Websites.aspx

Lawhelp.org: the place for you to find additional help & resources for your divorce in your area, including legal aid referrals
http://www.lawhelp.org/

Resources for Self-Represented Litigants: the place for you to find additional help & resources specifically if you are representing yourself
http://www.selfhelpsupport.org/help/item.Resources_for_SelfRepresented_Litigants

The American Bar Association Guide to Marriage, Divorce & Families: a general guide to many of the major issues and options in a divorce, for general background information
http://public.findlaw.com/bookshelf-mdf/

About the Author

Terry McNiff has been helping people see, picture, survive and thrive in divorce for more than 25 years. He has been teaching divorce attorneys to help people survive and thrive in divorce for more than 15 years. He has taught many hundreds of attorneys through many seminars, articles, and other writings over the past 15+ years.

Mr. McNiff wrote this book and made the pictures in *Picture Your Divorce* to help you see, picture, survive and thrive in your divorce – with your dignity intact.

Mr. McNiff provides divorce legal services to people in California, primarily in Southern California, including advising, consulting, counseling, co-counseling, serving as expert counsel re defined or limited issues, and representation. He also provides divorce consulting, brainstorming, and picturing services to people in need all over the world.

For a more complete list of the author's legal experience, and other pictures and tools to help you see and manage your divorce, please feel free to visit http://mcnifflaw.com or http://PictureYourDivorce.com.